OPEN DOORS

1950-1990

BAPTIST HERITAGE IN ATLANTIC CANADA

Documents and Studies

A Series Sponsored by

Acadia Divinity College

(Wolfville, Nova Scotia)

and

The Baptist Historical Committee

(United Baptist Convention of the Atlantic Provinces)

EDITORIAL COMMITTEE

Jarold K. Zeman, Chairman
 (Acadia Centre for Baptist and Anabaptist Studies, Wolfville, N.S.)

Philip G. A. Griffin-Allwood
 (Lawrencetown, N.S.)

Barry M. Moody
 (Acadia University, Wolfville, N.S.)

George A. Rawlyk
 (Queen's University, Kingston, Ont.)

Robert Wilson
 (Acadia Divinity College, Wolfville, N.S.)

Baptist Heritage in Atlantic Canada: Documents and Studies
A series sponsored by Acadia Divinity College
and The Baptist Historical Committee
(United Baptist Convention of the Atlantic Provinces)

PUBLISHED VOLUMES

1. **The Diary of Joseph Dimock**, ed. George E. Levy, 1979.
2. **Repent and Believe: The Baptist Experience in Maritime Canada**, ed. Barry M. Moody, 1980.
3. **The Journal of John Payzant**, ed. Brian C. Cuthbertson, 1981.
4. **The Journal of Henry Alline**, eds. James Beverley and Barry M. Moody, 1982.
5. **New Light Letters and Songs**, ed. George A. Rawlyk, 1983.
6. **Newlight Baptist Journals of James Manning and James Innis**, ed. D. G. Bell, 1984.
7. **The Sermons of Henry Alline**, ed. George A. Rawlyk, 1986.
8. **An Abiding Conviction: Maritime Baptists and Their World**, ed. Robert S. Wilson, 1988.
9. **The Memoir of Mrs. Eliza Ann Chipman**, eds. Allen B. and Carolene E. B. Robertson, 1989.
10. **Baptists in Canada 1760-1990: A Bibliography of Selected Printed Resources in English**, Philip G. A. Griffin-Allwood, George A. Rawlyk and Jarold K. Zeman, 1989.
11. **"Through Him Who Strengthens Me": Selected Shorter Writings and Sermons of Stuart Eldon Murray**, ed. with a brief biographical sketch by James S. Murray, 1989.
12. **Open Doors: Canadian Baptists 1950-1990. Popular Addresses and Articles** by Jarold K. Zeman, 1992.

Additional volumes in preparation.
The series is printed and distributed by Lancelot Press,
P.O. Box 425, Hantsport, Nova Scotia   B0P 1P0

OPEN DOORS

Canadian Baptists 1950-1990

Popular Addresses and Articles

by

Jarold K. Zeman

Introduction by George A. Rawlyk

Published by

LANCELOT PRESS

for

Acadia Divinity College and
The Baptist Historical Committee of the
United Baptist Convention of the Atlantic Provinces

1992

COPYRIGHT © 1992 by Acadia Divinity College

Printed and distributed by
>Lancelot Press Limited
P.O. Box 425
Hantsport, N.S. B0P 1P0
Canada

This volume appears with the generous assistance of the Jackman Foundation, Toronto.

ISBN: 0–88999–473–0

Table of Contents

Introduction by G. A. Rawlyk xi
Preface xiii
Editorial Note xv

PART ONE: EARLY SPIRITUAL PILGRIMAGE
    A.* My Conversion and Call to Ministry (1950) 3

PART TWO: MINISTRIES AMONG IMMIGRANTS
    B. Baptist Missions Among Czechoslovak People
       in Canada (1954) 15
    C.* Why Do Immigrants Come to Canada? (1961) 20
    D. The Role of the Ethnic Church (1964) 26
    E. The New Approach to
       New Canadian Work (1962) 34

PART THREE: EVANGELISM AND HOME MISSIONS
    F. Pathways to Better Evangelism in the
       New Century (1967) 43
    G. Are Canadian Baptists Interested
       in Social Action? (1967) 57
    H. Two Visions (1968) 62

PART FOUR: RENEWAL AND REVIVAL
    I. The Sleeping Giant (1967) 69
    J.* The State of the Convention (BCOQ) (1968) 73
    K. Believers in Expectation (1979) 77
    L. Can God Turn the Tide? (1982) 86
    M. Potential for Renewal (1985) 96

PART FIVE: CANADIAN BAPTIST HERITAGE AND IDENTITY
    N. The Courage to be a Minority (1966) 105

    O.* The Paradox of Baptist Origins
        and Destiny (1970) 112

    P. Authority and Freedom: A Baptist View (1970) 114

    Q. Building a Future on the Past:
        The Role of Historians (1990) 123

PART SIX: CANADIAN BAPTISTS IN THE WIDER ECUMENICAL CONTEXT

    R.* The Believers' Church:
        Who is a Believer? (1967) 132

    S.* The Significance of the Concept of
        the Believers' Church (1977) 135

    T. Growing Together (1980) 137

    U. Interfaith Interface (1984) 143

    V.* Report and Reflections on the Sixth
        Assembly of the World Council
        of Churches, Vancouver, BC, 1983 147

PART SEVEN: CONCEPT OF MINISTRY AND MINISTERIAL TRAINING

    W. How to Train Good Ministers (1957) 157

    X. Partnership in Ministries (1987) 163

    Y.* A Plea for Wholeness in
        Theological Education (1990) 170

APPENDICES

    I List of Abbreviations 178

    II Biographical Table 179

    III Bibliography of Selected Popular Publications 194

    IV Bibliography of Selected Scholarly Publications 201

    Pictorial Appendix 205

— — — — — — — —

*Published for the first time.

This volume is dedicated to

LILLIAN,

and to our children,

MIRIAM, DAGMAR, TIMOTHY and JANICE.

Their love, understanding,
support and sacrifices made possible
much of my service to others.

Open Doors

Behold, I have set before you an open door ....
                                    Revelation 3:8 (RSV)

The Lord has opened a door for me.
                                    2 Corinthians 2:12 (NIV)

And pray for us, too, that God may open a door for our message, so that we may proclaim the mystery of Christ .... Pray that I may proclaim it clearly, as I should.
                                    Colossians 4:3-4 (NIV)

INTRODUCTION

Early in his pastoral ministry, in the 1950s, Jarold Knox Zeman was visited by a distraught church member. Unable to deal adequately with her deeply-rooted psychological and spiritual problems, he advised her to see a medical doctor or a psychologist. "She looked at me," Zeman has noted, "with a mixture of disappointment and rebuke, and then, after a long pause of silence, she asked: 'Well, aren't you a man of God?'" This question would haunt Zeman for the next four decades and more. Was he, in fact, "a man of God, or just a practitioner of religion and theology?" This profound tension would significantly shape his varied Baptist ministries, as pastor 1949-59, Secretary of the Home Mission Board of the Baptist Convention of Ontario and Quebec 1959-68, as teacher at Acadia Divinity College, from 1968-91, and as a distinguished historian and scholar.

Those who know Jerry Zeman well will realize that, with God's help, he has succeeded in being both a "man of God" and an unusually gifted "practitioner of religion and theology." This inner tension, without question, has energized Jerry Zeman and at times, it would inspire, and also almost immobilize him. In a very real sense, Jerry Zeman was his own most severe critic. He expected so much from himself, often forgetting that he has accomplished so much in so little time. Despite a very heavy teaching and administrative load at Acadia, he, nevertheless, has served as a pastor to hundreds of students. And, moreover, he was a publishing scholar widely regarded in the historical profession as the leading authority on the Anabaptists and Czech Brethren in Moravia and Bohemia during the sixteenth and early seventeenth centuries. Zeman also played a key role in what has been recently called "The Renaissance of Maritime Baptist Studies." As chairperson of the Editorial Committee for the "Baptist Heritage in Atlantic Canada" Series, he has, with his tremendous energy and commitment, thrust the Atlantic Baptist experience into the mainstream of Canadian religious history.

In the articles which follow, Jerry Zeman has selected from the many popular addresses and papers he has presented since 1950, those which throw the most light on his various careers as pastor, administrator, teacher and prophet. Born on February 27, 1926, in Semonice, Czechoslovakia, Zeman had to endure the twin horrors of the Nazis and the Communists in his native land. His conversion and calling eventually led him to study for the Presbyterian ministry and to Knox College in Toronto. While in Toronto, after much soul-searching and after carefully studying the New Testament, Zeman became a Baptist. This was not an easy decision for this young Czech immigrant to make, and it would leave an indelible mark on the man and his ministry.

Zeman's articles about the Christian ministry among immigrants to Canada still strike a responsive chord. He understood and understands the immigrant experience, and his sensitive and prophetic message can still be read with considerable profit, even today. Though not a native of Canada, Zeman almost intuitively realized how important the historical past was in shaping the contemporary Canadian Baptist identity. Too few Canadian Baptists have unfortunately realized this important fact. Zeman fully appreciates the "Wider, Ecumenical Context" in which Canadian Baptists must locate themselves, and he certainly understands the strengths and weaknesses of "Ministerial Training" in contemporary Canada. In fact, one might have expected a little more criticism from Zeman—a person whose critique of theological education is well known and very perceptive indeed.

Zeman's Christian commitment, his considerable knowledge and wisdom permeate all of the articles which make up his *Open Doors*. This is a volume which possesses both prophetic insight and prophetic power. Canadian Baptists, alas, over the last half century, have *not* been strongly influenced by either prophetic insight or prophetic power. To remain strangely indifferent will, I am certain, push Convention Baptists, in particular, further and further into the dark periphery of Canadian religious life.

> George A. Rawlyk
> Queen's University,
> Kingston, Ontario
> December 24, 1991

PREFACE

The year 1991 marked the fiftieth anniversary of my initial commitment to Christ, and the fortieth anniversary of my commitment to Lillian in our marriage covenant. It also brought my retirement from the so-called "full-time" ministry. These occasions provided opportunities for recollection of, and reflection on, my life pilgrimage.

I was grateful to the members of the Editorial Committee of the "Baptist Heritage" series for their suggestion that I prepare a volume of selected articles and addresses which would exemplify the various stages of my service among Canadian Baptists. With some hesitation, I accepted the invitation.

The process of sorting out and selecting suitable texts was both a refreshing and a humbling experience. In retrospect, I could see more clearly than ever before how gracious God had been to me, and to my wife and family, when he kept opening for me so many doors to various ministries and leadership roles during the past four decades. In doing so, he worked through particular persons in Canada and abroad. Their names and faces remain stored in my memory as a precious treasure. They are too many to be listed here. At the same time, I realized over and over again how inadequate my responses to the perceived challenges had been.

I believe that the selected addresses and articles provide not only a concise record of my pilgrimage and ministries but also, and more importantly, a mirror of some of the trends, both theological and institutional, which shaped and modified the identity and role of the Baptist churches, related to the Canadian Baptist Federation, since 1950. And this, to my mind, is the main reason for the publication of this book. Subjective as all personal statements are, such eye witness accounts and individual insights can contribute to the ongoing search for a clearer understanding of Canadian Baptist identity and mission. They are also appreciated by historians as one of the essential sources for their task of describing and interpreting history. Most of the volumes, published in this series thus far, fall in the category of such personal documents, as diaries, journals, sermons, letters and hymns.

The twenty-five texts in this volume were chosen as a balanced selection which is representative of my ministries in three ways. (1) Each text is related to one of the seven major themes. (2) The texts are arranged in chronological sequence under each category. (3) The geographical coverage corresponds to the scope of my ministries. Items from all but three of the Canadian provinces, plus one each from Europe and the U.S.A., are included. In the biographical and bibliographical appendices the reader will find additional information.

In one respect, the volume is incomplete. In addition to addresses, lectures, and published articles or books, preaching has been the major, if not the central, means of communication in my ministry. I have preached in every Canadian province, in many states of the U.S.A., as well as in Europe. However, sermons should be viewed as a different and unique category of communication. As a proclaimer of the *kerugma*, an ambassador of Christ speaks with authority which can never be ascribed to any other expression of human opinion (cf. 2 Corinthians 5:19-20). That distinction, as well as the limited available space, led to the decision to exclude sermons from this volume.

I wish to express my appreciation to the members of the Editorial Committee for accepting my choice of the texts as a suitable selection of materials for this volume, and for approving its publication.

I acknowledge, gratefully, the permission to reprint any copyright materials, granted by the respective publishers, or by editors of periodicals. They are identified at the end of those selections where it applies.

I am also indebted to Mr. Gary Dunfield for his meticulous preparation of the text for publication, and to Mr. William Pope, and to Lancelot Press, for the production of the volume.

Wolfville, N.S.
December 31, 1991
Jarold K. Zeman

EDITORIAL NOTE

1. This volume contains "popular" addresses and articles. Scholarly publications are listed in the Bibliography (Appendix IV).
2. Materials which are published for the first time are marked with an asterisk in the list of contents.
3. At the end of each selection, an editorial note identifies the source from which the text is reprinted, and/or the occasion for which an address, or paper, was prepared.
4. The text of previously published materials is reprinted without changes, except for the correction of printing mistakes, and minor revisions in diction or style in order to clarify the meaning.
5. Consistency in spelling, such as the use of capital letters, applies only within each selection. The reprinted materials reflect the editorial norms of the various periodicals and other publications from which the texts are reprinted.
6. Deletions of parts of the text in any reprinted material are indicated by editorial notes.
7. Bibliographical references for quotations in the text have been kept to a minimum, and appear as endnotes with each text.
8. Permission to reprint any copyright materials was granted by the respective publishers.

PART ONE:
EARLY SPIRITUAL PILGRIMAGE

A. MY CONVERSION AND CALL TO MINISTRY (1950)

A Statement before the Examining Council for Ordination, Convened by the Toronto Association of Baptist Churches (Baptist Convention of Ontario and Quebec) at the Request of the Czechoslovak Baptist Church in Toronto, May 30, 1950.

Introduction

When our Czechoslovak Church was sending out the invitations for this examining, and possibly ordaining, council, the letter included three biblical texts:

The first one, from Psalm 119:94: "I am thine, save me! For I have sought thy precepts!"

The second one, written in I Cor. 9:16: "Woe is unto me, if I preach not the Gospel!"

And the third one, as recorded in the Latin version of the Scriptures, *MANET DEI VERBUM*, which may be translated: The word of God stands, or remains, or as expressed in the words of Peter (I Peter 1:25): "The Word of the Lord endureth forever!"

These three verses from the Bible sum up in a perfect way all that I am going to witness about: first, God's call and my response to become his son (conversion); second, God's call and my response to be the minister of his glorious Gospel; and third, what I stand for as a Christian Baptist minister (convictions).

1. Conversion: How God in his unsearchable mercy has called me to believe in Jesus Christ and to enjoy fully the certainty of eternal life.

I was the first-born in a teacher's family in a village in Czechoslovakia. My father's folks were Presbyterian

(Reformed) for generations, my mother's ancestors were Roman Catholic.

I was brought up in a warm atmosphere of a pure and precious parental love sacrificing everything for the benefit of their children. The only thing that lacked was the true Christian warmth. Although my mother became Presbyterian, the spiritual curse of a mixed marriage could not be done away with easily and quickly.

The school building we lived in was in the direct neighbourhood of the Presbyterian church and manse. My father was the organist and choir leader. Thus I had a good opportunity for an early musical training.

I had to attend the Sunday School but I often preferred to run away to my Roman Catholic grandmother in the opposite part of the village. She was quite sympathetic with such refugees from the heretical Sunday School.

I passed the Presbyterian confirmation when I was thirteen, with sincere admiration for the Reformation saints, and was given a Bible with the following text inscribed by our minister who was a true Christian man: "I am thine, save me! For I have sought thy precepts!"

I liked it but I was far from understanding it for "the natural man receiveth not the things of the Spirit of God" (I Cor. 2:14). I put the Bible into my library and did not care for it, nor for the young people's meetings, held in the neighbourhood of my home.

When I was attending High School the war broke out. A few weeks before Germany invaded the Soviet Union, on a bright last April Sunday afternoon 1941, God for the first time made me desperately hungry for his Word.

A tract of an evangelistic interdenominational society got into my hands and made my conscience feel very uneasy. The horror of sin and its wages (death) arose before my eyes to an extent that made me cry and despair. But his precious Word, recorded in John's Gospel, by the power of his Spirit brought his healing in a few days.

A: My Conversion and Call

The month of May 1941 came full of blossoms and beauty. I was the happiest man in the world – amidst all the dangers and horrors of war! God has called me directly through his Word. There was no human testimony mediating his call except the tract mentioned before.

There is nothing in this world like the first love of Jesus, especially when it is the love of a fifteen-year-old boy (or girl), even amidst all the May flowers of God's nature.

Then I understood my confirmation text: "I am thine! Save me!" He has saved me – my Saviour, my Lord!

2. Call to Ministry

To be born again really means to become a baby in Christ, whether you are 15 or 50! And the spiritual baby has to grow a lot in order to develop into "a perfect man... the stature of the fulness of Christ" (Eph. 4:13).

The nine years that have elapsed since my conversion in 1941 were not years of continuous joy. That of course was not God's fault but mine.

For two or three years following my conversion, I was a burning witness of my Lord, full of the enthusiasm of his Holy Spirit. The Presbyterian Church – more exactly a sort of a United Church embracing former Presbyterians and Lutherans – was the only Protestant church within my reach. So I had to use it as the channel for my missionary activities as Sunday School teacher and young people's leader.

Our new minister welcomed my cooperation except in one case. With a friend of mine I decided to distribute evangelistic tracts at school, at work and last not least, in our church. We succeeded everywhere except in the church. After we had placed the tracts in the pews before a Sunday morning service, the caretaker rushed in to remove the "dangerous" literature "threatening the unity of the church".

After the service, we were called before a special meeting of the elders and rebuked for an unsound zeal in distributing literature not officially approved by the church headquarters, and for holding ourselves for better than the other members of the church.

Such little incidents, together with a deepening knowledge of the Scriptures, necessarily brought me to the point of questioning the character of the Presbyterian Church. Out of the 1,000 members of our church only 100 - 120 were attending the church regularly, and that church was considered to be a good one! There was no church discipline whatsoever, no difference in life between church-goers and non-church-goers. Such and other observations hovered in my mind for months and years and led to the final conclusion that the conception and practice of baptism was the key to all these problems.

Meanwhile, however, as the war years passed, I went through the sad experience described in the second chapter of the Book of Revelation, namely, leaving the first love of Jesus. Gradually, the Word of God was loosing its sweet attractiveness for me. I could do without it for days. My devotional programmes in the Young People's Society were becoming more and more philosophical talks. Away from my heart was the joy of the Holy Spirit.

When I had to decide about my vocation after the end of the war, I chose the philosophical and philological courses at the University in Prague, planning to be a high school—or perhaps college—teacher. I was doing exceptionally well in the exams. But I was doing worse and worse in my mind and heart. Having the best chance to watch the post-war conditions in all spheres of life from the central city of Europe, Prague, where East and West at that time were meeting in a way never heard of before, the vanity and emptiness of the modern life began to dawn upon me in all its depressing aimlessness and shortsightedness.

What is the use of all intelligence and education for a generation of cynical murderers and hypocritical businessmen pretending to be full of humanitarian love and selling a man's life for a few cents without a remorse? There is no worth nor sense in such a life which people in the 20th century are lead-

A: My Conversion and Call

ing, or more exactly, suffering. And if there is no purpose in life why should I continue to bother myself and others by living?

There are only two consistent concepts of life: the one of the suicide, and the other, a wholly consecrated life in Jesus Christ. Most of the people to-day walk somewhere between. I am afraid that most of the church people do so too.

But only such a man or woman can walk on the very peaks of the mountains of Christian consecration who before has literally been led by God through the valley of the shadow of death.

The word "salvation" originally meant, both in Hebrew and in Greek, a rescue from the first, temporal death. The Gospel then revealed the true eternal nature of salvation.

In my short life God has saved me three times from the temporal death: First, in a hopeless pneumonia case when I was a baby; then, in a still more hopeless diphtheria case when I was twelve years old; and finally, when I contemplated suicide as a bright university student of twenty.

God has permitted me to pass through all of it to make me aware and conscious that I live only because he has saved me. He has saved me to use me exclusively for his own use and purpose, and he will permit me to live only as long as I am fulfilling his purpose.

Ever since my conversion I have felt the necessity of witnessing about my Lord to other people. But I did not wish to be a full-time worker. To be paid for the Gospel work is a stumbling block to many people, in Europe particularly. But God finally showed me that the Crucified Christ himself is the greatest stumbling block to such people.

During the summer vacation after my first university year I heard the call of my Lord clearly and distinctly: Thou art mine, wholly and entirely. Don't try to find excuses like Jonah did. Don't say, "People would not listen to me if I were paid for it," but follow the way of Amos confessing:

"I was no prophet neither was I a prophet's son, but I was a herdman. But the Lord took me and said unto me: 'Go, prophesy unto my people Israel!'" Follow the way of Isaiah who heard God's call, "Whom shall I send and who will go for us?", and replied: "Here am I! Send me!"

God began to lead me back to the first love of Jesus. It was no easy way. It meant "biting" myself through mountains of doubts. But God so loved me that he brought me back to himself.

I am thine, my Lord! Save me and keep me! I may have not been seeking thy precepts as I should have, but I am seeking them now. "Woe is unto me if I preach not the Gospel. Necessity is laid upon me."

In the fall of 1946, I left the philosophical faculty and entered the Hus Presbyterian Theological Seminary in Prague to prepare for ministry. Two years later I was granted a scholarship by the Reconstruction Committee of the World Council of Churches to pursue further theological studies at Knox College in Toronto. I graduated from Knox a year ago.

I was expected to return to my native country. All my biblical studies have led me to a firm conclusion that infant baptism was not scriptural and that it was the root of all other problems in the Presbyterian and United Churches. No man but the Word of God itself has made me a Baptist while I was still on the Presbyterian roll. What shall I do after I return to my own country and am sent to a church to perform the duties of a Presbyterian minister?

A few weeks before the ship was to sail I received a warning not to return. You can hardly understand what it means to cut off all cultural and personal ties one has been cultivating for more than twenty years in Europe.

That was a great decision. But another one had to be made, still more important: the decision to join the Baptist fellowship of Christian people.

In Toronto I took every opportunity to get in touch with different groups of Christian people. For the first time, I

A: My Conversion and Call

watched a baptism on profession of faith and by immersion in the Ossington Baptist church.

My heart was beating. The word was becoming flesh. The persons and events from the fifth book of the New Testament were being resurrected from the silent pages of the Holy Writ into our days. This is what I have been looking for through the years of my Christian life.

With a sad but firm voice, I shared my decision with my Presbyterian and United friends who were anxious to use me in their service. I loved them, and I still do. Some of them have called me traitor, others in the depth of their hearts feel in accord with my decision but they do not have enough courage to take the same step I did. They are aware as I was that either we have to obey the Word of God in every little detail, or stop declaring that we are a Reformation church having the Bible as our only guide and authority.

Although I could have entered the service on an English field I felt called primarily to serve the people who, like myself, left their home country and whom their insufficient knowledge of English prevents to draw the proper benefit from English services.

In fact, it is not a matter of language only. Even if I would speak a perfect English I would still be a European. Our mindset is in many ways different from the one the average Canadian-born person possesses because of the thousand years old traditions that have been molding us since our childhood, and because of the present day experiences we had to go through. All that necessarily finds its expression in the way of illustrating and presenting the Gospel to Czechoslovak and any other New Canadian people.

That is why I, at least for the beginning, considered it to be my primary task to proclaim the Gospel to the people of my own language and background. Rev. Joseph Zajicek, the first minister of the Czechoslovak Baptist Church, baptized me just a year ago, and I was received with an unusual degree of love and friendliness not only into the Czech church by also into the wider fellowship of our Baptist people in Toronto and throughout Canada.

Looking over the first year of my service in this church I feel happy and deeply thankful to God that he has led me this way.

Only a few months ago I learnt from my parents who still live in Czechoslovakia that in the days when I was dying from diphtheria at the age of twelve, they prayed and made a promise to God to dedicate me to his full-time service if he would save me from death. He did but they never mentioned to me their sacred vow, in fact they did not like my idea of becoming a minister.

But God has changed and transformed even their minds and hearts. I am so glad that at this moment, thousands of miles away, my father and mother — I am sure — are praying for their son and praising the name of the Lord for the gracious way in which he has fulfilled his own plans with me.

To use the words of Paul (Gal. 1:15): "It pleased God who separated me from my mother's womb and called me by his grace, to reveal his Son in me, that I might preach him among the heathen", be they the heathen of the twentieth century, in Toronto, or anywhere else.

3. Convictions

This is a sacred moment of disclosing the innermost motives which led me to take this stand before you to-day. Therefore, I am not going to present an outline of the Christian creed which you may read in any textbook of systematic theology.

Rather I shall make an attempt to stress a few points which to my mind are of greatest importance for a young man entering the full-time ministry of the Gospel in the middle of the twentieth century.

There will be four sections: 1. What is truth? 2. God and man. 3. The people of God (the Church of Christ). 4. God, his Church and this world.

A: My Conversion and Call

[Note: The text of this section is deleted here.]

Conclusion

Entering the ministry of my Lord and his church in the exact middle of the twentieth century, I am aware more than perhaps any other minister in Canada that I am taking upon me a burden which I myself shall not be able to bear.

But that is the proper starting point for the Christian ministry: to despair entirely about myself, about all my God-given abilities, may they be many, and to look to Christ, the Crucified and Risen One, in tears and smile: "I am thine! Save me, keep me, lead me, my dear Lord!"

When Paul and Barnabas were ordained in the church in Antioch, they were ordained with fasting, praying and laying-on of hands on the express command of the Holy Ghost: "Separate me Barnabas and Saul for the work whereunto I have called them!" (Acts 13:2). I do believe in the same call.

My ordination takes place in the same month of May, in which nine years ago he called me to be his; in the same month, in which just a year ago, he led me to seal my faith by baptism; in the very same month, in which three days ago, in the remembrance of the first Pentecost, he has reminded me of the only possible foundation for Christian ministry.

I pray and beg you to pray that either he may fill me abundantly with the irresistible power of his Holy Spirit, or else, trample me down in the very beginning that I do not run in vain. For there is no other way for a true minister of the Gospel of Jesus Christ.

Amen.

[Note. The text of this statement was prepared for oral presentation rather than for publication. All scriptural quotations are from the King James Version.]

PART TWO:
MINISTRIES AMONG IMMIGRANTS

B. BAPTIST MISSIONS AMONG CZECHOSLOVAK PEOPLE IN CANADA (1954)

The name of Czechoslovakia was almost unknown to the people outside of Europe until this small nation of 12 million people became a symbol of the life-and-death struggle between democracy and modern totalitarian movements: the small country was first sacrificed to appease the Nazi aggressor in Munich 1938, and ten years later, in February 1948, it was left to be the first victim of the Communist expansion.

1. In the Old Country

Tragical as these two events appear on the world scene they are even more challenging to one who is familiar with the history of the freedom-loving Czechoslovak people. In Bohemia, the most western province of Czechoslovakia, the continental reformation began its powerful proclamation of the pure Gospel and of the principles of a Protestant democratic society, by the fearless preacher John Hus. His martyr-death at the stake (1415) could not stop the country's adherence to the Scriptures. The nation became ninety per cent Protestant and through its exiled "Moravians" influenced the Zinzendorf movement in Germany and indirectly initiated the Wesleyan revival in Great Britain and North America.

At home, however, the Protestant majority, which in the sixteenth century included over 100 flourishing Anabaptist churches, was almost entirely suppressed by a fierce Roman Catholic counter-reformation after the peace treaty of Westphalia in 1648. That was the first "Munich" experience in Czech history. It took almost three centuries before the full freedoms were restored in the independent Czechoslovak Republic in 1918, only to survive for twenty brief years. Religiously, the people have not yet been awakened to return to the faith of their fathers. The nation is 75 per cent Roman Catholic, with well organized Lutheran, Presbyterian

(Reformed), and "Czechoslovak" (Unitarian-Episcopal) minority denominations. The Baptists in Czechoslovakia show but some 4,000 members. Nevertheless, they made important news in 1953 when several of the leading pastors were tried and sentenced to long prison terms by the present Communist government. One of them has since been tortured to death.

2. Immigrants

No wonder many Czechs and Slovaks left their country to seek more lasting freedom and better living conditions. There are almost three million people of Czechoslovak origin living outside Czechoslovakia today. A substantial majority of these live in the U.S.A. In Canada, there are about 75,000 residents of Czechoslovak origin, more than half of whom live in Ontario and Quebec. With the exception of farmers they — like immigrants of other nationalities — flock to a few industrial centres to create considerable and quite compact minority groups, such as those in Toronto (about 10,000), Montreal (6,000), Windsor (2,500), Hamilton (2,500), Vancouver (2,000), Winnipeg (1,500), Oshawa, London, Sarnia, Sudbury (500).

3. Baptist Missions Among Czechoslovak Immigrants in Canada

In their missionary service to immigrants, the Baptists of Canada have not overlooked the newcomers from the country of John Hus. Although intensive work among Czechoslovak immigrants did not begin until in recent postwar years, it has reached thousands of newcomers and old settlers most of whom are nominal Roman Catholics with little or no interest in religion. Hindered by indifference or fanatical enmity against the Baptist "sectarians", the Czechoslovak missions have, nevertheless, made considerable progress: There are two churches in Western Canada: Winnipeg (25 members) and Minitonas (250 members) and two organized churches in Ontario: Windsor (55 members) and Toronto (85 baptized members plus some 400 "associate" friends in more or less regular attendance). The Czechoslovak group in Montreal,

B: Czechoslovak People in Canada

meeting since 1952 under the ministry of Rev. J. Zajicek, will be organized as a church in the near future. Besides, there are several other points in Ontario, such as London, Hamilton, Batawa and Oshawa, where regular or occasional Czechoslovak services are being held.

4. Special Methods of Work

Since there are practically no Baptist people among Czechoslovak immigrants, new members can only be added through conversions from among nominal Roman Catholics or Protestants. All possible means of contacting the newcomers are being devised and tried.

The importance of "first contact" with the perplexed immigrant upon his arrival in the Canadian port of entry can hardly be over-stressed. Port work done by Rev. J. Zajicek in Montreal and Quebec, and other missionaries in other harbours, has persuaded many an unchurched immigrant to attend a church in Canada.

Social work, undertaken on a large scale particularly by the Czechoslovak Bethlehem Baptist Church in Toronto, might grow into a burdensome task at times. Yet all of its channels, such as the emergency hostel in the Sunday School section of the Toronto church for newly arriving or long unemployed immigrants, assistance in seeking suitable employment and accommodation, interpreter's function, etc., not only introduce the Baptist "brotherhood of love" to a lonely and lost immigrant but should also be acknowledged as an unparalleled service to the country in shaping the opinions and attitudes of future Canadians.

Educational work ranges from the regular S.S. and B.Y.P.U. program in some New Canadian churches to special projects undertaken by the Toronto Czechoslovak church, such as: a school for New Canadian children on Saturday afternoons; a reading-room in the church, open on all days, with some eighty Christian and secular papers and magazines both in English and in Czech; a lending library; classes in English; special Y.P. weekend conferences; their own summer camp program in Camp Huronia at Lake Simcoe where 45 New Canadian children between 7 and 15 years spent two weeks of wonderful recreation and Christian training in August 1954; seventy per cent of them were from non-Baptist homes; some of them were in Canada for less than a month; many read the Bible for the first time.

Gospel work in the sense of preaching, visitation and personal evangelism is the crown of all church work. Some 4,000 Czechoslovak people were approached with the Gospel in the Toronto area alone since 1949. In January 1952, twenty people accepted Christ in one meeting, and sixteen of them were baptized a month later. Ordinarily, however, decisions for Christ and church membership come very slowly and require long years of patient ministry of word and love. "Herein is that saying true, one soweth, and another reapeth" (John 4:37).

5. Czechoslovak Baptist Congress in Toronto, 1954

A top event in the life of Czechoslovak Baptist missions in Canada was the Czechoslovak Baptist Congress held in Toronto for an entire week in July 1954. Some 120 accredited delegates of Czechoslovak Baptist churches from across Canada and the U.S.A. together with over 700 guests attended. At this Congress, held under the patronage of two prominent Canadian federal cabinet ministers from Ottawa, the delegates solemnly confirmed their loyalty to the full Gospel of Jesus Christ as the foundation of the great historic Baptist principles; they re-affirmed their ties with Canadian and American Baptist conventions and with the Baptist World Alliance; they also expressed sincere thanksgiving to God for freedom in their new homeland and deep concern and intercession for the suffering Church in their native land. The Congress launched a vital program of radio-evangelism among the Czechoslovak immigrants all over the world, even reaching the people in Czechoslovakia.

"Ye shall know the truth and the truth shall make you free."

B: Czechoslovak People in Canada

[Reprinted from a pamphlet under the same title; Toronto, 1954.]

C. WHY DO IMMIGRANTS COME TO CANADA?

(A Sermon on C.B.C. "Church of the Air" Service, July 2, 1961)

This weekend marks Canada's ninety-fourth birthday. It is perhaps significant that the church service on this occasion originates in one of the one hundred New Canadian Baptist churches; that the prayers of gratitude for our wonderful land come to you from the hearts and mouths of men and women most of whom have lived but a few years in this country. Could it be that the majority of immigrants appreciate the privileges of life in Canada more profoundly than the native citizens who so often take their birthright for granted? Or, to quote the eloquent words of the Irish-born Canadian journalist and statesman, Thomas D'Arcy McGee, one of the Fathers of Confederation, who wrote, almost a hundred years ago:

> Dear, most justly dear to every land beneath the sun, are the children born in her bosom and nursed upon her breast; but when the man of another country, wherever born, speaking whatever speech, holding whatever creed, seeks out a country to serve and honour and cleave to, in weal or in woe—when he heaves up the anchor of his heart from its old moorings, and lays at the feet of the mistress of his choice, his new country, all the hopes of his ripe manhood, he establishes by such devotion a claim to consideration not second even to that of the children of the soil.

Why do immigrants choose to come to Canada? There seem to be three main reasons. Some come seeking *security*, and therefore opportunity for a higher standard of living. Back in their native lands of Europe and Asia, the storms of our days have made everything insecure. Houses were destroyed, factories demolished, farms confiscated, families

C: Why Immigrants Come

torn apart. Canada, with her untapped resources and waiting opportunities, beckons to such people like an island of refuge would to shipwrecked voyagers.

Then, there are others who have come to Canada in search of *freedom*. I shall never forget the overwhelming sense of freedom I had during the first few months after my arrival in Canada. In contrast to the everpresent government imposition upon one's personal affairs in my native land, no one here seemed to be concerned about who I was, or what I was doing. Most of us soon realized that freedom implies not only freedom from coercion but also freedom for creative living. Among the citizens of this country, no one would echo more conscientiously the words of our Prime Minister [John G. Diefenbaker] than the political refugees of the twentieth century: "I am a Canadian, a free Canadian, free to speak without fear, free to worship God in my own way, free to stand for what I think right, free to oppose what I believe wrong, free to choose those who shall govern my own country. This heritage of freedom I pledge to uphold for myself and all mankind."

There is yet another reason for the coming of many newcomers to Canada. Immigration to them is a way of *escape* from some unpleasant situation, be it family or marriage strife, business failure, or even a disappointed love affair. Their desire to make a radical break with the past, and to make a fresh start in Canada, usually affords the promise of a satisfying career. One might do well in recalling the life story of Joseph Scriven, the author of the familiar hymn "What a Friend we have in Jesus" who decided to leave Dublin for Canada because his fiancee had drowned only a few days prior to their wedding date.

Something happens to all immigrants after they have spent a year or two in Canada. The old nationalistic prejudices and hatreds subside and appear ridiculous. The class distinctions of the old European society are worn off. We are all witnessing a miracle: a new nation is being born before our very eyes. It is being born in our schools, community groups and in many of the churches.

Open Doors

Let us not, however, be carried away by cheap enthusiasm. No miracle in the true sense of the word can happen by mere human action. Racial, cultural and social integration will not, by itself, produce a new nation. Nor will some new Canadian nationalism, of whatever flavour it might be, melt the contrasting groups within our population into the unity of a people.

What is needed is a radical transformation of the very nature of men and women as human beings. What do we mean?

The vast majority of immigrants, whether from Great Britain or from the Continent of Europe, come with a background of *nominal Christianity*. There are exceptions, of course. We have welcomed to our shores thousands of consecrated Christians whose knowledge of Scriptures, devotional practices and loyalty to the church of their fathers are admirable. Unfortunately, so many of them remain in self-enclosed fellowships, thus preventing a wider influence upon Canadian life. For most newcomers, however, their contact with the church in Europe was limited to a few ceremonial occasions. Their knowledge of the rudiments of Christian doctrine is shockingly shallow. They have had no personal experience of the power of Jesus Christ as Saviour from sin and Lord of all life.

In an interview with an American journalist some years ago, the President of Argentina remarked: "When I ponder about the similarity of the continents of North and South America, when I realize how equal our natural resources and yet how contrasting our standard of living I can find but one explanation. Our continent was originally settled by the Spanish who came here in search of gold. Your continent was settled by the Pilgrim Fathers who came in search of God." Such an analysis would hardly apply today.

The three reasons for immigration to which we referred earlier, clearly indicate a spiritual vacuum in the minds and hearts of most New Canadians. Some of them come seeking material security and fail to realize that nothing in this world,

C: Why Immigrants Come

not even in Canada, can be regarded as secure. Jesus Christ alone remains the same yesterday, today and forever.

They come as escapists from a past which is stained with the fruit of sin. Yet no distance can erase the memories of moral bankruptcy, nor lift the burden of guilt. Only Christ can do that for you and for me. He alone, the Lamb of God offered on the Cross, will lift your burden, cleanse your unclean heart, forgive your rebellion against God. All you need to do is to look up to him in prayer: "Father, in the name of your Son Jesus, forgive and cleanse me. Accept me as your child."

The same Christ offers also true freedom. For no man can consider himself free until he is made free from the powers of evil by the indwelling Spirit of the Risen Lord. Mere freedom from outward political coercion can degenerate into license. A person enslaved by his or her passions is not a free person. The powers of evil are too strong for any one of us to cope with. Only as we, through personal faith, receive the Person of the Living Christ and surrender our will to his will, do we become free. The apostle John writes: "Behold the Lamb of God who takes away the sin of the world. To all who received him, who believed in his name, he gave power to become the children of God. God gave us eternal life and this life is in his Son."

What we have said about New Canadians applies to a large number of other Canadians as well. The churches are plagued with nominal adherents of Christianity. Many Canadians are unchurched altogether. There is no greater task the churches in Canada can perform for the good of this country, in obedience to the divine commission, than to lead people through the experience of a personal reconciliation with God and one another.

With the apostle Paul we say: "In union with Christ Jesus you who once were far off have been brought near through the shedding of Christ's blood. Thus you are no longer aliens in a foreign land, but fellow citizens with God's people, members of God's household" (Eph. 2:12-19).

Open Doors

[Note: Of the many verbal and written responses to the radio program, the following two merit inclusion here.]

Acadia University July 3, 1961
Wolfville, N.S.

Dear Mr. Zeman,
Many thanks for your broadcast yesterday. I was glad that I had no callers to distract my attention.

To me it was what such an address ought to be — in content, in phrasing, in relevance and in delivery. The emphases, both in place and in tone, of themselves gave meaning to the message.

We enjoyed the singing also. May God richly bless you and your work.

Yours fraternally

F. W. Patterson
[President, 1923-48]

National Religious Advisory Council July 4th, 1961
of the Canadian Broadcasting Corporation
Toronto, Ontario.

Dear Dr. Zeman:

I write personally and on behalf of the National Religious Advisory Council to thank you, your fellow ministers who helped in the service, and the choir leaders and choirs who contributed so wonderfully to the musical portions

C: Why Immigrants Come

of an order of worship that was very well planned and presented.

You and your associates enabled a great many Canadians, and I assume not a few Americans, to understand more deeply, the Lordship of Christ. This was the theme of the beautiful selections with which the service opened and this theme was well maintained, to the end of the service.

I am sure that the many fitting references to Canada's birthday and to the hopes and contributions of those who have come recently to live in this new land combined to make the service a very fitting remembrance of Dominion Day.

Please express to those who helped you the gratitude of the National Religious Advisory Council.

Kind regards

Yours sincerely,

J. R. Mutchmor
Secretary.

D. THE ROLE OF THE ETHNIC CHURCH (1964)

When immigrants try to relate themselves to the religious life in Canada, they are confronted with a fourfold choice: (1) They can join one of the existing churches (an "indigenous" Canadian church — if there be any such denomination in Canada: all except the United Church of Canada were imported by migrants!). (2) They may establish an ethnic congregation within an indigenous church. (3) They may form a separate ethnic church (a new denomination). (4) They may lose contact with the church and become "unchurched".

What is an "ethnic" church? Is it synonymous with a "language" church? In the past few years, it has become customary to call ethnic churches in Canada "New Canadian" churches. The name implies a congregation composed of new immigrants. The basis of their "togetherness" (*congregatio*) is their common ethnic origin. Their most obvious distinguishing mark is the language used in services and other phases of church life. The Roman Catholic Church in Canada can boast of the highest number of languages employed in its ethnic parishes. Baptists in Canada serve immigrants in fifteen different languages (in 1964) which is probably the widest range of languages shown by any Protestant denomination.

Should there be ethnic churches at all? The typical attitude of an English-speaking Protestant can be summed up by the question: "Why do they not learn English? Why do they perpetuate a foreign language in Canada?"

A more serious objection can be raised from theological rather than linguistic and nationalistic presuppositions. If it is true that "Christ has broken down the middle wall of partition" (Eph. 2:14) so that "there is neither Greek nor Jew, Barbarian nor Scythian . . . but all one in Christ Jesus" (Gal. 3:38 and Col. 3:11) what justification is there for a Christian church which chooses to live in ethnic segregation? Is not such a church a denial of the power of the Gospel?

D: The Ethnic Church

1. The Ethnic Church in the Context of Its Ethnic Community

The linguistic and theological reservations stated above fail to take into account the sociological context within which most ethnic churches in Canada live and function, namely, the ethnic community. Whether one views the Canadian pattern of immigrant settlement with approval or with misgivings, one must recognize the fact that in our cities and across the countryside there are immigrant communities of common ethnic origin.

Each of these settlements—"Little" Italy, Ukraine, Germany, Chinatown, etc.—represents a more or less complete culture which has been transplanted from "the old country" to Canada. Depending on its vitality and size, the ethnic community surrounds the newcomer with a miniature replica of his former homeland.

There are restaurants where he can enjoy the traditional meals. There are social clubs, national halls, libraries, and schools where children are taught the mother tongue of their parents. Most communities publish one or more newspapers, organize festivals and summer camps. If the community includes prosperous men who provide employment for their compatriots, an immigrant can settle in Canada and live his entire life in the "ghetto culture" of his ethnic group.

Should such a complete ethnic culture be deprived, arbitrarily, of Christian witness and fellowship? Should not the church be an indigenous part of every culture? From the viewpoint of missionary strategy, it is imperative that the Christian Church be at the very heart of every ethnic community in Canada.

In spite of the relative isolation of ethnic communities from Canadian life, one can detect the influence of Canadian pluralism. Very few immigrant communities are religiously homogeneous. In addition to the church of the majority which enjoyed, as a rule, the status of a state church in the homeland, there are smaller congregations of the Protestant evangelical tradition. Ministers of all ethnic churches, "established" and "nonconformist", enjoy a high social status within the community and receive public recognition.

Religious diversity is only one example of the process of stratification within each ethnic community. Gradually, each ethnic settlement, through the centrifugal force of integration into Canadian society, develops "an inner circle" and an "outer circle" — and several circles inbetween.

At the core of the community are the leaders — often former politicians — who consider the preservation of their national culture as their sacred duty. Then there are those who, because of no, or limited, knowledge of the English language, are completely dependent on the ethnic community for their living and social life. But there are also those who have become "citizens of two worlds": as New Canadians they still enjoy the festivals and concerts of their native culture yet more and more they tend toward English-speaking (or French-speaking) Canadian society. Finally, there are immigrants for whom the use of the mother tongue is no longer the necessary medium of preserving and passing on their ethnic heritage. Using English or French as their main language, they look at their particular ethnic culture as one shining piece in the total "mosaic" culture of Canada. Their ethnic community regards them as fringe members.

The ethnic community might be compared to an onion. It has many layers. The ethnic church should be related to all of them.

2. The Ethnic Church — An Anchor for the New Immigrant

In addition to its function within the ethnic community, a New Canadian church plays a crucial role in the personal life of the new immigrant. Through the initial weeks and months of his life in Canada, the church becomes an island of linguistic refuge. Here he can understand people and be understood. The church serves also as an anchor of psychological security. Self-confidence is regained, complex of

D: The Ethnic Church

inferiority vanishes, for a while, at least. The ethnic church becomes the centre of social life as well as an information centre, a counselling centre and an employment bureau. Many immigrants have their mail sent to the address of the church.

More than anything else, the ethnic church is the most effective *evangelizing* agency among new immigrants. The problem of communicating the Gospel to people of other lands and cultures has been one of the central problems of the modern missionary movement abroad. New Canadian work represents nothing less than overseas missionary work brought closer to home. The problem of communication is not resolved by translating a message into another language.

No language can be divorced from its total cultural milieu. A New Canadian pastor — if he truly communicates the Word of God to his people — uses illustrations and modes of expression quite different from those employed by Canadian ministers. A true missionary is fully identified with the people to whom he brings the good news of redemption. He understands their former defeats and victories; he knows of their national as well as individual sins; he shares their sorrows and hopes, memories and dreams. In order to reach the whole man, the Gospel must be presented in the thought forms and in the experiential context of the people to whom it is being communicated.

For the *new* immigrant, no one can do it better than an ethnic church. An ethnic church is more than a language church.

3. The Ethnic Church — Trapped in Isolation

An old Latin proverb states that the corruption of the best things results in the worst things. It applies to the ethnic church.

The particular social environment within which each congregation bears its witness, provides both the opportunity for effective service and the threat of a trap. Any church, be it suburban, town or rural, may become trapped.

Open Doors

Unless the ethnic church takes resolute steps toward gradual integration into Canadian religious life, it cannot avoid the trap of a *double isolation*. Most immigrants retain and cherish the memories of their homeland *as it was* when they left it. As time goes on, their image of the homeland and its culture becomes obsolete. It is little more than a dream.

Unless there is continuous mass migration from a particular country, the immigrant loses contact with his homeland. Nor is he in touch with the rapidly changing culture of North America. He becomes isolated from both cultures and lives in an imaginary world.

The story of the Hutterite and Mennonite colonies in Canada is well known. The Mennonite churches are beginning to leave their religious and cultural reserves. But many other ethnic congregations and parishes — Protestant, Eastern Orthodox, and Roman Catholic — are trapped in a gradual stagnation to death. Neither nostalgic nationalism, supported by religious crutches, nor religious messianism grounded in ethnic ambitions, can serve as the basis for a vital mission.

The more evangelical ethnic churches are exposed to an additional danger. In their emphasis on separation and consecrated life, they refuse to become involved in parties and other social events of their ethnic community. Before they realize it, they are regarded by their compatriots as "outsiders." Due to lack of identification with the ethnic community, their witness is ignored.

4. The Dual Involvement of a Healthy Ethnic Church

Very soon after its establishment in Canada, an ethnic church or congregation should seek a dual involvement in culture. For the newly arriving immigrant, the ethnic church serves as the natural orientation point. The names which many ethnic churches choose, such as the names of the patron saints of their homeland, or of the famous cathedrals and chapels, indicate that the church may become the very symbol of ethnicity.

D: The Ethnic Church

However, in a few years' time, the second generation begins to make its influence felt in the ethnic church. Children and young people who were brought to Canada early in their life, or who were born here, do not and cannot have the same ties with the "old world" traditions as their parents. They are Canadians. Some of them revolt against the "non-Canadian" patterns of their parents.

A healthy ethnic church will, therefore, attempt to relate its life both to the ethnic community and to Canadian life. At the right time, neither too early nor too late, the English language should be introduced into some phases of church work. If a continuous flow of immigrants of a particular nationality ceases, the ethnic church faces an alternative. Either, it will gradually identify itself with the Canadian religious scene, retain its young generation and incorporate into its fellowship persons of other ethnic backgrounds, mainly through intermarriage, or it will preserve a religious culture that is no longer relevant nor needed — with the final result of losing most of its young people and, one day, closing its doors. The two paths open to ethnic churches have been demonstrated again and again in the U.S.A. and in Canada.

On the whole, Protestant ethnic churches integrate into Canadian church life faster than the Roman Catholic and Greek Orthodox parishes. Most Baptist New Canadian churches maintain a dual affiliation: with the Baptist Convention in Canada and with an ethnic conference which comprises all Baptist congregations of the same ethnic origin located in Canada and, usually, in the U.S.A.

5. The Future of the Ethnic Church in Canada

We have been using the term "ethnic church" rather loosely. In most cases, we have referred to ethnic congregations which are related to an existing indigenous Canadian denomination. Since 1945, new ethnic churches, that is denominations, have been established in Canada only by the Protestant immigrants from the Netherlands (the Christian Reformed and the Dutch Reformed Churches which are branches of the mother church in the U.S.A.) and by immigrants of the Greek or Eastern Orthodox confessions.

Practically all Protestant ethnic congregations are affiliated with one of the Canadian Protestant churches. To what extent are such congregations involved in the main stream of Canadian Protestantism?

No comprehensive data of research are available. Many ministers who initially served ethnic churches become pastors of English-speaking congregations. As for the varied patterns of co-operation and integration, the ethnic congregations may be classified by the following categories:

1. Monolingual churches — the initial stage.

2. Bilingual churches — a gradual introduction of English alongside with the mother tongue of the immigrants.

3. Churches of All Nations — pioneered by the United Church of Canada; a number of ethnic congregations use the same building under the general supervision of an English minister; all groups join in an English service.

4. Twinned churches — an autonomous ethnic congregation meets in the building of the English congregation; gradually, additional areas of co-operation and integration are introduced.

5. Integrated Churches — a complete organizational merger of an ethnic church with an English-speaking church; an ethnic pastor might be retained to minister to the older immigrants.

6. Channelling churches or "feeder churches" — the ethnic church is seen from the beginning as a mission which wins converts and establishes contacts with immigrants but later channels them into regular English congregations.

7. "Ethnic missioner" approach — an ethnic minister works among immigrants without organizing an ethnic church; such work is usually a joint project of several local English churches and the Board of Home Missions. The ethnic missioner may use several buildings as the base of his work and he himself serves in the capacity of an assistant pastor in

D: The Ethnic Church

several congregations. Example: the Italian Baptist missioner in Toronto.

[Reprinted from *The Whole World at Our Door* (Toronto, 1964), pp. 11-15.]

E. THE NEW APPROACH TO NEW CANADIAN WORK (1962)

The number of immigrants who have entered Canada in the fifteen postwar years now exceeds the two million mark. More than half of the newcomers establish their residence in the province of Ontario. More than 20 per cent settle in the western part of the province of Quebec, chiefly in Montreal. It is obvious that the Baptist — and all other — churches in Ontario and Quebec face a major missionary task. The cumulative effect of postwar immigration upon the total life of our society, particularly in the large urban centres, is yet to be understood by the majority of our churches.

I The Two Patterns of New Canadian Work

In the past two or three decades, the Baptists in Ontario and Quebec have been aware of the missionary challenge presented by the continuous flow of newcomers to our cities and countryside. However, apart from the cursory contact provided by port workers, we have limited our missionary outreach among New Canadians to two main channels: the ethnic church and the Canadian Christian Fellowship work.

The Ethnic Church

The merits and demerits of an ethnic church which carries out all or most of its ministry in the native tongue of the newcomer, have been discussed frequently. In terms of meeting human needs and bearing an intelligible witness to the new life in Christ the ethnic church renders a service which could hardly be replaced by any other type of church or social agency. This pertains especially to the initial period of the newcomer's adjustment and with respect to some ethnic groups and certain types of immigrants. Under the auspices of the Home Mission Board the Gospel is now being proclaimed regularly in eleven languages (in addition to English and French).

E: The New Approach

In recent years, the Board has pursued the policy of placing one New Canadian Church with an English-speaking congregation in the same building rather than gathering several New Canadian groups by themselves in one building, or encouraging any New Canadian church towards acquiring its own church edifice. Such a policy works towards a better mutual understanding and provides for a smoother integration.

The Canadian Christian Fellowship

No historian will be able adequately to assess the heroism and persistent patience with which many individual women, and not a few Baptist Women's Mission Circles, addressed themselves to the difficult task of helping and reaching New Canadians. From the early thirties, the B.W.M.S. in Ontario and Quebec has sponsored the "Canadian Christian Fellowship" groups. Full time lady missionaries and countless volunteers have organized teaching centres of English, and in addition, they have taught thousands of lessons in homes; they have kept up visitation and created friendship groups for lonely immigrant domestic workers.

Depending on the power of God released through the Prayer Partner Movement these brave souls entered dwellings in urban and rural districts which had been given up by ministers and congregations. They surmounted the barriers of background and language. Theirs was a true ministry "from heart to heart," and frequently "from hand to hand" in providing material assistance to people in need. The vision and courage of these workers is matched only by missionaries on overseas fields.

II The New Approach

A Task for the Whole Church

With the increased immigration in the postwar years and the urgent need for Canadian men to reach New Canadian men, it became obvious that neither the few ethnic churches nor the small women's groups can cope with the expanding mission field at our doorstep. The incredible amassment of newcomers in the large cities and in some rural districts shifts the responsibility from a few concerned individuals to the whole congregation.

The local church should make a study of and decide upon (a) a new organizational basis for its New Canadian work and (b) a program of training its members for New Canadian evangelization.

A New Organizational Basis

In the local church, the Board of Deacons (or the Church Council where in existence) should assume the general oversight of New Canadian work and delegate the responsibility for its particular phases to the different groups and organizations in the church.

The deacons might initiate a canvass of the neighbourhood in order to discover all unchurched New Canadian families and individuals. The task of contacting the homes might then be divided between several groups, e.g. the B.W.M.S., B.Y.P.U., Church School classes and men's groups.

If a teaching centre in contemplated, the church—through the Board of Deacons—should appoint the director. The responsibility for organizing and staffing the centre might be assigned to the Christian Education Committee, the Missionary Committee or the Evangelism Committee, in each case working in close liaison with the Women's Mission Circle.

Similarly, the deacons, or the congregation as a whole, should select and authorize leadership for a Friendship Group or any other New Canadian project. Such sponsorship will make it possible for the leaders to enlist both men, women and young people for New Canadian work. One of the handicaps under which the Mission Circles pursued their Canadian Christian Fellowship work in the past was the lack of co-operation from men and young people.

E: The New Approach

A Program of Training

No one would ever conceive of sending missionaries to foreign lands without extensive training which enables the missionary to understand the people and their culture. Yet on the home base, we have only too often assumed that Canadian Christians, both volunteers and fulltime missionaries, can reach, without any specialized training, the newcomers from other lands with cultures so different from ours. Such procedure is both illogical and irresponsible. Canadian churches which plan any type of New Canadian work should, first of all, provide training for their people, "the home missionaries."

A minimum course of training should include the following units:

1. Understanding the Background of the particular ethnic groups represented in the community. Countries of origin differ greatly in their historical and cultural traditions, economic standards, social customs and religious life. Nothing could be more dangerous for a New Canadian worker than to make hasty generalizations. A group of workers might meet for a series of meetings in which they will study one country at a time. Any public school teacher, or a good high school student, should be able to gather the basic information from an encyclopedia or a reliable travelogue.

2. Understanding the Motives for Migration. Canadians often ask the question: Why do immigrants come to Canada? The reasons for leaving one's homeland and choosing Canada as one's adopted homeland vary from case to case, or at least, from one national group to another. While immigrants from poverty stricken regions of Southern Europe obviously come for economic reasons, others, such as Hungarian freedom fighters and other political refugees, come in search of freedom. Others might seek escape from some frustrating family situation, or come in pursuit of sheer adventure. Many immigrants follow the trail started by one member of their family clan.

3. Understanding the Process of Integration. However sincere and well-meaning a Christian might be in his endeavour to help the newcomer, he will be of little use unless he can discern the problems of adjustment which confront the immigrant. A group of prospective church workers should discuss the linguistic, economic, social, cultural, moral, psychological and religious adjustment of the newcomer.

It is more realistic to speak in terms of "integration" rather than "assimilation." Integration suggests a two-way process. Immigrants adjust to Canadian society and Canadian society adjusts, to some extent at least, to the immigrants and accepts some of the colour, flavour and customs, as well as ideas and skills, the immigrants have brought with them.

4. How to Reach the Newcomer. Practical instruction should be provided for those who will visit in homes, or those who will teach English. The psychology of friendship might be discussed as well.

5. How to Share Our Faith with the Newcomer. This is the foremost goal of all our New Canadian work. After we have befriended the immigrant and extended help to him, ought we not to introduce him, or her, to our best Friend, Jesus Christ, the Saviour and Lord? Personal faith in Christ and an individual responsibility to Him is at the heart of the Canadian Protestant way of life. Without such a personal relationship to God the whole moral structure of our society will collapse. Both the eternal destiny of the individual immigrant and the national destiny of Canada are at stake. If we fail to evangelize the immigrants most of whom come to us with a background of nominal Christianity and indifference to the church, we shall fail our God, betray the great spiritual heritage of this country and bear the tragic consequences of a secular, disintegrating society which will, in turn, call for coercive political measures. The sooner we realize the far-reaching implications of New Canadian evangelism the better service we shall render to Christ as Saviour of individual persons and Lord of nations.

There seems to be, in the minds of many Protestant Christians in North America, a false concept of bearing witness to Jesus Christ.

E: The New Approach

Many people decided that while they might continue as believers in Christ they would never be caught dead telling anyone else about it. They are determined to be discreet and quiet about their faith, to let their lives speak, if any speaking was required, and to avoid, at all costs, forcing their opinions upon anyone else... Testimony must be in both deed and word. The spoken word is never really effective unless it is backed up by a life, but it is also true that the living deed is never adequate without the support which the spoken word can provide. This is because no life is ever good enough. The person who says naïvely, "I don't need to preach; I just let my life speak," is insufferably self-righteous. Which one among us is so good that he can let his life speak and leave it at that? ... There has to be a verbal witness because there cannot be communication of important **convictions** without language. "I cannot be being good," says Samuel M. Shoemaker, "tell of Jesus" atoning death and resurrection, nor of my faith in His divinity. The emphasis is too much on me, and too little on Him. "...We make a witness by telling not **who** we are but **whose** we are.[1]

While these words written by Elton Trueblood in 1961 apply to the task of witnessing in general they have a particular relevance for witnessing to New Canadians. Too many well-meaning Baptist people stop short of the greatest deed of kindness they should render to their New Canadian friends: to point them to Christ. How will they ever see the need for a personal acceptance of Christ—in place of a dim reliance upon church ceremonies and good deeds—unless the basic terms of the Gospel are clearly explained to them?

Endnote

1   Elton Trueblood, *The Company of the Committed* (New York: Harper and Brothers, 1961), pp. 46 and 53-54.

Open Doors

[Reprinted from a pamphlet under the same title; Toronto, 1962.]

PART THREE:

EVANGELISM AND HOME MISSIONS

F. PATHWAYS TO BETTER EVANGELISM IN THE NEW CENTURY

An Address Presented to the Baptist Federation of Canada in Assembly in Ottawa, Friday, July 7, 1967

Introduction

No other aspect of the life of the church has received more attention in recent years than the task of evangelism. No doubt this is an indication of the concern about the apparent failure of the church to fulfil its central task.

The word itself has become one of the ambiguous terms into which one can read any meaning. We do not intend to survey the trends in contemporary evangelism. We shall avoid references to the many new books which discuss the renewal and mission of the church and are, therefore, relevant for evangelism. Those who are familiar with the literature on these subjects will recognize our indebtedness to such authors as Elton Trueblood, Robert Raines, Alan Walker, Wallace Fisher, Donald Miller, George Webber, Colin Williams and many others.

We propose to deal with the task of evangelism in the particular context of Canadian Baptist churches, especially in Ontario and Quebec. Our aim is *to erect a few road signs* which might serve to guide the subsequent panel and group discussions at this assembly and hopefully, also in the local churches. Accordingly we have revised the title of our address to read "Pathways to Better Evangelism in the New Century."

The main part of our presentation (Part III) will introduce a series of juxtapositions of *concepts expressed in a dialectic creative tension*. This method of discussion might be compared to the practice of the department of highways whereby both sides of the road pavement are marked with a white border line. If you wish to avoid the ditch—especially in foggy weather—stay between the two border lines.

Much of the contemporary discussion of evangelism seems to have taken on the form of pushing towards one-sided alternatives. We feel that at least some of these are not genuine alternatives. They do not represent a choice, "either - or." They must be held together in a creative synthesis, *"both - and,"* or replaced, in some cases, by a new solution.

I - The Canadian Baptist Context

As Canadians we are entering the second century of our political existence as a nation in the midst of a revolution. In fact we are involved in *several simultaneous revolutions*. The impact of the profound changes is being felt more in some parts of the country than in others. But no area is exempt from its effects. What are these revolutions?

1. We are experiencing, first of all, revolutionary changes in the composition and distribution of our population. The three major sociological trends may be described as *urbanization, immigration* and *mobility* (migration within the country but also "vertical" mobility in terms of social status). The average Canadian family changes its place of residence every fourth year.

The following figures will indicate the rate of urbanization. According to the 1966 Census statistics, released a few weeks ago, 65 p.c. of all Canadians live within the boundaries of 325 urban centers (villages, towns and cities) with population over 5,000. Fully 48 p.c. of Canada's population now lives in 19 metropolitan areas, each of these with population in excess of 100,000. The migration towards the metropolitan areas is best indicated by the fact that these 19 centers accounted for 71 p.c. of the net gain in Canada's population during the five-year period 1961-1966.

2. These changes have in turn accelerated the *cultural revolution*. In one generation, the cultural outlook of this country will have changed from a traditional culture, permeated and dominated by the influence of the Protestant or

F: Pathways to Better Evangelism

R.C. churches, into a *secular culture* independent of, or even hostile to, the churches.

3. The transition to a secular society is marked by an *ideological revolution* which is also related to the technological (scientific) revolution. The theme of EXPO '67 is a fitting expression of the philosophy of humanism: "Man and his world."

4. These changes in our society are bound to produce shock and confusion within the churches. The response of the churches has been, in most cases, one of two:

Traditionalism ignores or rejects all or most of the new concepts and tries to operate with old views and methods.

The *"cult of change"* worships everything new as long as it is different from the past.

A speaker at a recent conference which I attended said: "I am all for trying out new things. But let us not discard the old squeaky boats which we have been paddling along until we are sure that the new ones will stay afloat."

5. As a further complication in the process of adjustment to the emerging new patterns of society, our churches are caught in *the dilemma of Canadian ecumenicity*. The ecumenical relationships in Canada have been, and are being determined both by sociological and by theological factors.

In terms of *"social ecumenity"* Canadian Baptists have gravitated, for several decades, towards the large Protestant denominations: Anglican, Presbyterian and United. We share with them a similar middle class outlook and identical educational standards for the ministry. Family ties created by intermarriage usually point to the same denominational links. We have enjoyed the prestige of being included, as a rule, among the "four major Protestant denominations" although such an assumption can now be challenged on the basis of census statistics. All of these are undeniable facts of social ecumenicity.

Yet, at the same time, if we have any consciousness of our historical origins and theological convictions as Baptists,

Open Doors

we know that in terms of *"theological ecumenicity"*, our immediate ecumenical links are to be sought elsewhere in the Christian family. Our closest spiritual brothers and cousins are not Episcopal and Presbyterian churches with their concepts of infant baptism, "mixed church membership" (committed believers and nominal members) and with their respective forms of church government, but rather such denominations as the Disciples, the Mennonites, Associated Gospel Churches, other groups of Baptists and many others. With these we share a common understanding of the church as a fellowship of believers which is constituted on a non-creedal and non-sacramental basis. But we must confess that in spite of such theological affinities, our practical ecumenical contacts with these groups have been minimal.

This is our dilemma: The strong pressures of social ecumenicity have almost annulled an ecumenical solidarity in terms of theological principles. We have soft-pedalled our convictions to such an extent that in the eyes of the public we have lost identity. When Canadians make their choice of denominational affiliation, they turn either to the "big" Protestant churches with their minimal membership requirements, or to the smaller groups with their unapologetical expression of convictions, and warm fellowship. Our churches which stand somewhere "inbetween" are bypassed.

We may pride ourselves in the fact that because of our "middle-of-the-road" position we have a significant contribution to make to the ecumenical movement as a whole. This could be so if we had a clear witness to bear. But our "neither-nor" position has hardly helped our evangelistic outreach. That is why the dilemma of ecumenicity has been included in our discussion.

6. We are thankful for the evidences of *a new evangelistic concern* manifested by many of our pastors and congregations. It should be pointed out that at least in the Convention of Ontario and Quebec the lamented lack of numerical growth can be traced, to some extent, to the honest "cleaning up" of the membership rolls. According to the Yearbook statistics, the membership gains through 20,844 baptisms during the

F: Pathways to Better Evangelism

years 1953-65 were nearly offset by 15,404 erasures reported for the same period of time. These figures would indicate a promise of net growth for the future but they also underline the urgency of "reclamation evangelism." We must learn how to reclaim inactive members and how to effect prompt transfer of members who move to other areas.

II - The Crisis in Evangelism

It is necessary to discuss yet another aspect of the wider framework of evangelism. A twofold crisis is affecting contemporary evangelism.

1. Crisis in Communicating the Gospel. By and large, Canadians in 1967 feel that paradise has been recreated in our affluent society. On the surface, at least, most people would deny the inner emptiness of their lives — which is one of the inevitable by-products of a materialistic civilization — and show little interest in "spiritual values."

In evangelism, we are offering "goods" which are wanted by very few people today. Apparently, they do not feel the need of "new life," let alone "eternal life." Modern man has developed a "bungalow" philosophy of life according to which all things that matter happen on one level only. Humanism as a man-centered philosophy of life, has no use for God and heaven "upstairs", nor for hell "below."

The crisis that we face in communicating the biblical Gospel to modern man is the discrepancy between his one-dimensional humanistic outlook and our "split-level" terms of reference which include a dimension of eternity and the transcendent realities of God and of the powers of evil.

The problem will not be solved by mere modernization of our *language* (imperative as this is). The most demanding task is the interpretation of the *meaning* of such biblical *concepts* as faith, hope, love, kingdom, grace, cross, righteousness, resurrection, new birth, and many others.

2. Crisis in Motivation for Evangelism. Perhaps a more serious crisis still, has developed within the church itself. What are the motives by which the contemporary Christian is persuaded to be an ambassador for Christ? Is the "concern for the lost" sufficient motivation? What does it mean? This is not a paper on the theology of evangelism. Nevertheless, the need of a clear theological basis for evangelism, cannot be over-emphasized.

a) *The (Eschatological) Motivation of Hope.* In its ultimate purpose, biblical evangelism seeks to introduce the eternal dimension into man's temporal life. Through the miracle of new birth, man becomes a child of God "to enjoy fellowship with God forever". Evangelism which loses sight of the eschatological consequences of a personal relationship with God has lost the vision of the Eternal God Himself.

What is needed today is the ability to recapture the *cosmic* dimensions of God's redemptive plan. The personal salvation of an individual must be seen within the wider cosmic framework. Like the contemporaries of Paul, modern man has a real consciousness of the world's destiny. He cannot avoid it in an atomic age.

In the providence of God, human and cosmic history is moving towards its ultimate fulfilment in the return of Christ, the realization of His Kingdom and the "new heavens and new earth", the new creation. The personal destiny (salvation) of an individual believer is only part of this dramatic conquest of the powers of darkness by the Risen Christ. The future belongs to the Christians. Those who now reject Christ exclude themselves from the eternal fruits of His victory. They can have no hope. The biblical categories of "life" and "lostness" (as motivation for evangelism) should be understood in this total framework.

b) *The Motivation of Love.* The "love motive" and the "hope motive" are two sides of the same coin. If I have any genuine love for fellow men then I will do all I can to introduce them to Jesus Christ so that they may become part of the new creation (II Cor. 5:17). I will seek to demonstrate such love by giving myself to fellow men even as Christ gave himself for the world.

III - Some Creative Norms for Evangelism

We shall now erect several sets of "road signs" pointing the way towards better evangelism. These norms should help us overcome the temptation of one-sided and mutually exclusive emphases.

1. The task of evangelism is defined in the New Testament **both in the indicative and in the imperative moods.**

a) *Evangelism as an Indicative.* No genuine Christian can avoid being an evangelist. The very style of his life bears witness to the presence of the living Lord in him.

"You *are* (not: should be, must be, or "be!") the salt of the earth."

"You *are* the light of the World ..." (Mt. 5:13ff.).

"I am the vine, you *are* the branches. He who abides in me, and I in him, he it is that bears much fruit ..." (John 15:5).

"You *shall* receive the power...and you *shall* be my witnesses..." (Acts 1:8).

"I have appeared to you for this purpose, to appoint you to serve and bear witness..." (Acts 26:16).

"If any one is in Christ, he *is* a new creation..." (II Cor. 5:17).

The clue to evangelism is not program but people, that is, Christians who follow criteria and values different from those of the society around them. The presence of such persons who live in continuous communion with God, reflects the power of Christ. The question to ask is:

Am I not too much concerned about *what I do* instead of being concerned about *who I am*?

If a survey of religious preferences had been taken in Rome in A.D. 65, the results would have likely shown 51 p.c. for Jupiter, 30 p.c. for Zeus, 9 p.c. for Mithhra... and 1 p.c. for Jesus. Did Paul give up? It would help us if we were more pre-occupied with the quality and depth of our Christian life than with the statistics on denominational growth, or lack of it.

b) *Evangelism as an Imperative*. Evangelism is also a matter of obedience. There are biblical imperatives which we must hear and follow.

"As you go, proclaim: The kingdom of God is at hand ..." (Mt. 10:7).

"Go, make disciples of all nations ..." (Mt. 28:19).

2. Evangelism in the Life Rhythm of the Congregation. The polarity of "being a Christian" and "obeying His commission" applies also to the life of the local congregation.

a) *The Gathered Church*. The healthy life of a local church is characterized primarily by sharing (KOINONIA). The larger the congregation, the more difficult this becomes. We have to admit with shame that many members of service clubs have a more meaningful experience of sharing than the "participants" in a Sunday service. We must discover such forms of congregational life which will make it possible for the individual Christian to share his daily spiritual life with fellow believers. One example of such sharing are *small groups* which can be gathered in homes, in places of work, in church buildings, or elsewhere. Retreats are also helpful. Integration into a life of sharing is essential for new converts as well as for fringe members. Cf. the proverbial "onion" concept of church membership: the inner, thinner and sinner circles.

Some congregations have been reconstituted on the basis of a covenant which demands certain minimal disciplines, e.g. daily Bible study and prayer, regular attendance of worship services and cell groups, involvement in at least one type of service within the church and another one in the community, and financial support.

b) *The Giving Church*. The sharing fellowship of a church becomes sterile unless it serves as a preparation for witness and service to the community at large. The life of a congregation is marked by the rhythm of gathering and dispersion.

3. An evangelical church is **both a redemptive (healing) and a prophetic community.** The two large conferences which were held in 1966 symbolize the polarity of modern evangelism: *"to save souls"* and *"to save society"*. Under the auspices of "Christianity Today" and under the personal chairmanship of Billy Graham, a World Congress of Evangelism met in Berlin. Earlier in 1966, a conference on Church and Society had been convened in Switzerland by the World Council of Churches (WCC).

Many Christians are tempted to regard these two approaches as mutually exclusive options. We are concerned either for the salvation of individuals or for the redemption of society as a whole. In the Bible, both concerns go together and it is only fair to stress that both Billy Graham and the sponsors of the WCC conference did underscore the need for a "both-and" approach.

a) The church is a *healing (redemptive) community*. In contrast to the highly individualistic mystical and spiritualist religions, the life of a Christian disciple is life in community. The local church provides a supporting fellowship for the modern man who is being crushed by the pressures of the depersonalized urban society.

b) The church is also a *prophetic community*. Jesus Christ is Lord over all. His kingship must be applied to all spheres of life. Individual Christians and churches cannot keep silent on issues of justice, equality and human rights. Silence and neutrality often mean betrayal of the Lordship of Christ. Witness within the "power structures" of society is part of the prophetic calling. One might speak perhaps of "preventive evangelism". As Canadian Baptists we have been strangely silent on public issues in recent years.

4. Evangelism seeks **the redemption of the whole person, body and soul.**

Luke 4:18-19 The theme text of Jesus' own mission.

Mt. 11:4-6 The evidence of His messiahship.

Mt. 10:7-8 The mission to the whole man.

a) *Kerugmatic Evangelism*. Evangelical churches have majored on evangelism as a verbal communication of the KERUGMA, the message of salvation.

> Testimony must be in both deed and word.... No life is ever good enough. The person who says naïvely, "I don't need to preach; I just let my life speak", is insufferably self-righteous. Which one among us is so good that he can let his life speak and leave it at that? ...There has to be a verbal witness because there cannot be communication of important convictions without language. "I cannot by being good", says Samuel Shoemaker, "tell of Jesus' atoning death and resurrection, nor of my faith in His divinity. The emphasis is too much on me, and not enough on Him." (Elton Trueblood).

Unless the church has a clear message of the Gospel, its witness degenerates into mere social work.

b) *Diakonic Evangelism*. By the same token, Christ expects His followers not only to present a message but also to demonstrate His presence and power through acts of service (DIAKONIA). Words are often poor substitutes for deeds. But deeds cannot replace words.

We should be aware of a temptation to which some congregations in North America are yielding. They become frustrated by their fruitless efforts in leading persons to a decision for Christ. Then they turn to social action where quick visible results can often be assured.

5. Evangelism is both spontaneous and organized.

a) *Charismatic Witness*. The power of the Holy Spirit is *the* condition of true witnessing (Acts 1:8; 9:17-20 etc.). Christians will use every opportunity for "spontaneous" witnessing under the guidance of the Spirit. Furthermore, some Chris-

F: Pathways to Better Evangelism

tians are equipped with the charismatic gift of "an evangelist" (Eph. 4:11).

b) *Organized Programs of Evangelism.* But such liberty of the Spirit does not preclude the necessity of a strategy for evangelism, both in the local church and in the denomination. Under the guidance of the Spirit, Jesus, Paul and others followed a definite strategy of outreach. It should be remembered that the charismatic gifts for the total ministry of the church include gifts for administration and organization (Rom. 12:8 and I Cor. 12:28f.).

Evangelism does not "just happen" in the local church. It should be planned on a year-round basis just as Christian education and other programs are planned. One of the most urgent needs in our churches is the wisdom of *setting goals* for Sunday School attendance and for making new contacts ("prospects"). We cannot set goals for the number of conversions but we can set goals for the number of new homes and persons whom we shall seek out and to whom we shall witness. The Holy Spirit who is the actual evangelist will honour our expectant faith. There will be decisions for Christ!

6. Crisis and Continuity in Evangelism.

a) *Crisis.* Life is made up of little and big crises, i.e. moments of decision. Modern man, especially, lives in a climate of crisis and decision-making. It is legitimate to expect of every mature person to make an initial commitment to Christ as Saviour and Lord, and to experience subsequent deeper commitments or surrenders. Ample opportunities should be provided in the life of the church for such decision making.

b) *Continuity.* Such moments of crisis must be seen in the context of the continuing life of the individual (and of the church). Healthy evangelism relates the experiences in commitment to the process of Christian education.

7. Methods of Evangelism

We have delayed the discussion of methods until the end of this paper. The reasons should be obvious. In keeping with the pragmatic outlook of North American culture ("Does it work?" "*How* do you do it?") our churches have been preoccupied with methods and techniques of evangelism. We feel that the basic principles and motives for evangelism deserve our foremost attention at this point in our history. If we know *what* our mission is and *why* we must pursue it, we shall find answers to the question "*how*". There is no scarcity of practical handbooks on methods of evangelism.

The basic rule was spelled out by Paul: "I made myself all things to all men *that I might by all means save some*" (I Cor. 9:22). There is no general methodology of evangelism which will work in every situation. We shall make brief comments on several methods which merit our special attention at this time.

a) *Residential and Non-residential Contacts*. The main bases of operation for church evangelism have been the church building and the home (residence). Visitation evangelism and other methods related to the residential context of life should *not* be discarded.

However, modern men (and many women!) spend far more time, and experience more meaningful involvement, in the non-residential contexts of their *work and leisure* than in the limited context of the residence (suburban bedroom communities). Evangelism must operate, therefore, more and more in the non-residential contexts. A decision for Christ made in such a context will likely be more costly and will represent a commitment in depth (the framework of total life). This approach might also provide us with one answer to the problem of reaching high-rise apartment dwellers.

b) *Mass Media of Communication*. If we are persuaded that Baptist churches must continue to bear a witness in the new century, we should give consideration to a speedy development of some nation-wide Baptist *radio and TV programs*. These need not be expensive half-hour programs such as the Lutheran or Mennonite Hours. Brief "spot announcements" (with a striking message or testimony) released on tapes and video-tapes for use on local stations might be one of the answers. In addition, some pastors and lay people

F: Pathways to Better Evangelism

should receive professional training for radio and TV ministry.

When we employ the radio and TV media we have an opportunity to address a person in the privacy of his home, hotel room or car. This form of evangelism is so *urgent* that it should receive *top priority* attention by all three conventions even if its implementation might mean the elimination of some other projects.

c) *Cooperative Evangelism.* Evangelism is, first and foremost, a witness to Jesus Christ and an invitation to receive Him and to follow Him. Wherever such witness and invitation can be extended through cooperative channels we should participate. There are many areas where cooperative action on *denominational* basis is needed. There should also be more evangelistic witness on an interdenominational basis, e.g. witness rallies and preaching missions.

d) *New Canadian Evangelism.* With the increasing influx of immigrants, many of our churches should undertake more extensive work among newcomers. As Baptists, we have had an excellent record of mission to immigrants. We proclaim the Gospel across Canada in more languages than any other Protestant denomination. The fastest growing congregation of the post-war era in the Ontario-Quebec Convention has been the Estonian Baptist Church in Toronto.

However, we face a new urgency in this area of opportunity. Some congregations will be forced to leave their present location unless they succeed in evangelizing immigrants and developing a church which is indigenous to their changing neighbourhood.

See also the booklet, *The Whole World at Our Door.*

e) *Evangelism and Church Extension.* It will likely be impossible for any denomination, let alone a small one such as ours, to keep up with the "sprawl" of our cities, and provide new church buildings in all major suburban areas. The prohibitive costs of construction (plus the likelihood of taxation on church properties) make it imperative that we rethink our extension strategy in the new century. Might it not be wiser for *some* new congregations to use rental premises, such as space in a shopping plaza? In some metropolitan areas, we should probably think in terms of "church centers" which would replace some of the uneconomical older church buildings and combine, in multiple purpose buildings, rental units such as apartments, stores and offices, with modern facilities for church work. In some areas, we may want to experiment with a cluster of house churches (e.g. in high rise apartments) related to one central large church.

Other new ways of evangelism could be mentioned. However, these few examples are sufficient to indicate how exciting and indeed adventuresome evangelism in the new century will be!

NOTE: In this paper we have avoided discussion of the crucial role of the laity in the task of evangelism. "The Place of the Laity in the New Century" will be the subject of another address.

Conclusion

"The company of Jesus is not people streaming to a shrine, and it is not people making up an audience for a speaker. It is labourers engaged in the harvesting task" (Elton Trueblood).

Jesus said: "I came to cast fire upon the earth." Commenting on this saying Leslie Newbiggin writes: "To be a Christian is to be part of that fire – to burn for His sake and share in setting the world on fire."

We have attempted to describe a few pathways which may lead us to better evangelism in Canada's new century. From all that has been said it should be obvious that in our opinion the key to faithful evangelism is the *person* who bears witness rather than a program or method.

[Reprinted from *The Report Volume of the Eighth Assembly of The Baptist Federation of Canada, Ottawa, July 6-9, 1967*, pp. 53-58.]

G. ARE CANADIAN BAPTISTS INTERESTED IN SOCIAL ACTION? (1967)

Within our own ranks and from our friends outside the denomination, we often hear the question, Why do not Baptists show more interest in social action? Is there something inherent in the Baptist theological position, in the very genius of the Baptist movement, which prevents the denomination from becoming involved more meaningfully and effectively in social service?

I suspect that among us, there are some who are inclined to answer this question in an affirmative way. They feel that, somehow, our emphatic insistence on soul liberty — as opposed to ecclesiastical and societal mediation and control of religious life — makes us, in a positive way, concentrate on personal evangelism and missions, and by the same token, in a negative way, neglect, if not shy away from any persistent interest in social action.

In his recent book, *The Industrial Struggle and Protestant Ethics in Canada*, Stewart Crysdale summed up his review of the minimal Baptist contribution in this particular area of social concern, viz. the Christian witness and service in industrial life and in labour-management relations, with the following words:

> The traditional stress upon the individual regeneration, the intense belief in personal liberty, the congregational basis of authority, and the doctrine of strict separation between church and state have prevented the Baptist denomination in Canada from playing an active and creative part in the process of social reform. Indeed, its reluctance to favour any one group in the power struggle has tended to dull its witness to righteousness in concrete situations, and thus it has failed to

defend the weak at critical points of struggle against the combinations of the strong.

On the other hand, Baptist churches have been zealous in an imperative and pure witness to the absolute separateness of the Gospel and at the same time its basic relevance to all human relationships. Their distrust of all earthly orders has deterred the churches from becoming identified uncritically with any humanitarian configuration. It remains to be seen whether the Baptist convention churches will be able to solve their own dilemma and bring a positive social witness to bear upon the serious remaining problems of Canadian industrial society. (p. 125)

Elsewhere in the same book (p. 116), Crysdale singles out the Baptist "distinctive doctrines of individualistic regeneration, ecclesiastical decentralization and polarity with the state" as the major factors in the Canadian Baptist disengagement and seeming disinterest in social issues.

We would question whether the explanation offered by Mr. Crysdale and others who share his view, is theologically persuasive and even historically accurate.

We must remind ourselves and our friends that the first attempt to deal with social issues in an organized fashion goes back to 1906 when the Convention appointed a "Committee on Temperance and Moral Reform". It was renamed the "Committee on Moral and Social Reform" two years later.

It should be noted that the formation of this Baptist Committee sixty years ago antedated the appointment of a similar committee by the Presbyterian Church in Canada (1907) and the Methodist Church in the U.S.A. (December 1907). The latter has since become the most vocal advocate of social action on this continent. The Committee on Moral and Social Reform of this Convention had an early start but its work did not keep pace with activities of similar committees in other denominations.

G: Social Action

In 1928, the Board of Social Service was organized. In 1941, its name and scope of work was enlarged to include evangelism. In 1944, the board published a booklet, *Toward a Christian Social Order*. In 1953, the sequel of names in the official designation of the board was changed to give priority to evangelism (The Board of Evangelism and Social Service). In the reorganization of the Convention in 1964, social concern was joined together with missions to specialized areas, such as Urban and New Canadian work, to form a Division of Missions and Social Action in the Department of Canadian Missions. In the process of further streamlining in 1965, social action was remarried to evangelism to form the present Division of Evangelism and Social Action.

Meanwhile, the Baptist Federation of Canada came into existence. Its Social Service Committee has shown sporadic efforts to jolt Canadian Baptists into cooperative steps in social action. Its main accomplishment seems to have been the publication of a helpful manual, *The Church and Social Problems* by Wm. G. Black.

A detailed review and analysis of all pronouncements and reports on social concern which can be found in the Yearbooks and in the denominational papers over the past sixty years would constitute a worthwhile project of research. But even a cursory examination of the records reveals that the fruit of the six decades is very meagre.

With one or two exceptions, we have not provided, as a Convention, a single institution for social welfare, such as a home for senior citizens, for unmarried mothers, orphans, or for released prisoners. Our local churches have entered into few projects of social service. We have avoided the practice of making bold pronouncements on controversial moral and social issues. The question is: Why?

Rather than blaming our theological position, I would like to suggest several practical reasons for this seeming lack of social concern.

(1) Some of our most capable men have entered interdenominational agencies and rendered invaluable services

Open Doors

there. The Rev. Fred N. Poulton became the first secretary of the reorganized Christian Social Council of Canada in 1950. Several of the general secretaries of the Lord's Day Alliance and the temperance movements have been Baptists. We have provided more than our share of leadership in cooperative social action.

(2) As a small denomination, we cannot allow our man power and material resources to be dissipated in a large number of projects. We must choose priorities. Up to the present, our major priorities seem to have been missions (especially overseas, where we are involved in many institutional projects of social service) and higher education (Moulton College, Woodstock College, Feller College, McMaster University). The fact that both the American Baptist Convention and the Southern Baptist Convention, with their massive resources and contrasting theological views, have been engaged in an impressive display of social service, demonstrates beyond any shadow of doubt that the Baptist doctrinal position as such cannot be blamed for lack of social concern.

(3) There is another way to assess the Baptist contribution to social action, not in terms of institutions but rather in terms of personal services. A considerable number of Baptist people, lay people and ministers, are involved, and have been involved for years, in projects of social service, either on a voluntary or professional basis. If some one could compile a directory of all such persons, it would be a noteworthy list indeed.

Most of them help with projects which are sponsored by interdenominational or community agencies. We are referring to work done by volunteers in such fields as Hospital Auxiliaries, Children's Aid Societies, Ontario and General Hospitals, correctional institutions and downtown missions, as well as to services rendered by professional social workers, probation officers, and others. In many cases, our people are not even identified as Baptists.

It is difficult to decide whether, as a denomination, we should deplore this practice, or encourage it. Are not Chris-

G: Social Action

tians meant to be the leaven of society as a whole? Or are we anxious to find satisfaction in the little Baptist lumps of social work here and there?

*   *   *

This brief discussion of Canadian Baptist involvement in social action has been prepared exclusively against the background of the Convention of Ontario and Quebec. Before one might attempt to answer the question, whether or not Canadian Baptists are interested in social action, one would have to survey also the situation in Western Canada and in the Atlantic Provinces.

However, as a preliminary conclusion we would suggest that Canadian Baptists are interested and involved in social action more than one has generally assumed. Furthermore, we would predict that interest and active participation will increase in the years that lie ahead.

[Reprinted from *Canadian Baptist Home Missions Digest*, Vol. 7 (1966-67), pp. 89-91 and 97.]

Open Doors

H. "TWO VISIONS":

DR. JAROLD K. ZEMAN AT TORONTO B. W. CONFERENCE, MARCH 25, 1968

[NOTE: A report by Miss Alfreda Hall, Editor of *The Link and Visitor* (May 1968 issue, pp. 151f.)]

Dr. Jarold K. Zeman, Secretary of the Department of Canadian Missions in our Convention, was the guest speaker at the evening Conference of the Toronto Baptist Women, held in Kingsway Church, March 25, 1968. When the date was set, there was no hint that Dr. Zeman's resignation was pending and that this would probably be his last official address to B.W.M.S. groups. Although the announcement of his appointment to the Faculty of Acadia University's Divinity School had not yet been made public, the news had spread so that friends from all over the city gathered to hear him.

The usual inspiring features of the meeting took second place to the speaker and his message. The reporter's task is not to reproduce it in detail but to record its significance and to try to convey something of the spiritual power and compelling urgency of the occasion.

Dr. Zeman began by paying tribute to the Mission Circles, thanking them for opening the doors of outreach and witness to newcomers and especially for their "unceasing ministry of prayer" on behalf of the work of Canadian Missions. He spoke of addressing the B.W.M.S. on various occasions. Many memories were stirred. Some of his hearers suddenly realized that they had been, over a period of nineteen years, witnessing the development of a great Christian leader. They had welcomed Jerry Zeman to the Baptist fold after his theological studies at Knox College and conversations with Rev. J. Zajicek. They had seen him hesitantly commencing his missionary work among his compatriots and at Beverley St. Church, Toronto, and then, with increasing power of leadership, as pastor of Bethlehem (Czech) Congregation. They had rejoiced in his marriage and growing family and had wel-

H. Two Visions

comed him to the pastorate of the historic church at Villa Nova, now set among newcomers. They had delighted in his appointment as assistant to Dr. Burns, and had watched his maturing growth through studies at Ruschlikon-Zurich. Finally, they had felt satisfaction as he stepped capably into the influential office of Secretary, combining tasks of administrator and pastor of many churches. As these memories, mellowed with thoughts of his generous, radiant spirit, flashed across their minds, his friends were thankful for his ministry among us.

As Dr. Zeman's address on "Two Visions" unfolded, the importance of his contribution to our church life was clearly revealed.

He spoke of "earthly" matters, and one recognized his profoundly practical yet imaginative outlook on the problems and witness of the Church in the coming years.

Referring to an account in the press of the Utopia that is expected in the year 2000, "only 32 years from now", he pointed out that much leisure will bring more misery, doubts of the purpose of life, and mental illness. Having lived through the Nazi and Communist revolutions in Czechoslovakia, he feels that the gradual one in which we now live is more subtle and dangerous: what we have believed to be right and true is now declared to be false, and our convictions are undermined. This revolution is accelerated in three ways: urbanization brings great materialism; immigration brings newcomers with a religionless philosophy or with Christless religions; high mobility takes away all constancy and stability of society. Canada is a young nation: half of the population is now under 25 years of age; one-third, under fifteen years of age.

What does this mean in a practical way to the churches? In rural areas it may not be possible any longer to have a church in every town. Churches should, perhaps, follow the school plan and have one central church in a district with modern equipment and the best of facilities for worship and teaching. In the Inner City, churches should consolidate and gear their work to this area. The pulse of the city will be found here where high-rise developments will concentrate more people who will develop a new type of culture. Crucial locations in the city should be kept; suburban dwellers should drive back to them to work in clubs for young people, and similar types of outreach. The tradition of the old church building must, perhaps, be cast off; on its valuable site a high-rise building must replace it, much of the space being rented to commercial or residential interests, but the church retaining its place in their midst. In the suburbs it will be impossible to keep up with the rapid residential expansion; cells of believers meeting and worshipping in homes and clustering around one big church may be an effective outreach. When the longer days of leisure come, it will be possible for the preacher to spend this time in ministering to the flock and during working days to follow a secular occupation.

Such was the vision of the "exciting era that will call for boldness, fearlessness, and minds open to experiment while retaining allegiance to the old powerful message of the Gospel."

Dr. Zeman gave a special word of encouragement in the teaching of newcomers, "a most urgent mission field": "Do not get tired of teaching and visiting. It pays off! ... Launch out to work with new groups, Asian and African... The test of your real missionary fervour is only now coming. You have done much for foreign lands; you are going to have to prove your sincerity here at home."

He mentions ideas that are still only dreams: a Friendship Centre for drifters, a Halfway House for those who must be rehabilitated to enter society, a Hostel for Canadian Indians; and of some that have begun to materialize: Programs for Senior Citizens, centres for practical aid, a Home of the Aged. "We need," he said, "to move more aggressively into preventive work. We need to give sacrificial service in political and public life, to demonstrate Christian conviction in the power structures of society where decisions affect the lives of men. We need to be more and more sure that urban renewal and improved economic environment will

H. Two Visions

not change people; that the centre of change is not disguised social action, but evangelism."

The warmth and dynamic of Dr. Zeman's own experience of "the heavenly vision" was seen in his references to the personal nature of our missionary task. He showed how the Scriptures stress the fact that we are not saved for ourselves alone but to serve and to witness to Christ. This involves love for people, identification with people, becoming "all things to all men". It means that a church should become Italian in order to serve Italians, and that traditions should be set aside so that our churches may become attractive to other types of people. It means that each believer must respond to God's call by saying, "What do you want me to do?" — "What can I give of myself to others for Christ's sake?" — "How can I, through the leading of the Holy Spirit, discern trends and use my Christina witness as He appoints?" Again and again, the speaker stressed the urgency of one person witnessing to another. He concluded with this moving incident:

A Hindu student from India, studying for two years in Toronto, said to his professor before leaving: "My people feared for me to come to study in a Christian land ...But no one in Canada has ever said a word to me about Christ."

"What kind of mission business are we in," he asked, "if we send money and men to India, but have no word for the man from India who comes to our land?"

And again, "When last did you try to lead someone to Christ? It is the only way by which a Baptist church can grow."

[Note. This digest of a message is included in this volume as an example of how popular addresses were received and interpreted by audiences. The other comments by the editor, Alfreda Hall, provide a context for the departure from Central Canada for the teaching ministry at Acadia Divinity College in July 1968.]

PART FOUR:

RENEWAL AND REVIVAL

I. THE SLEEPING GIANT (1967)

"In all this, remember how critical the moment is. Now it is high time to awake out of sleep: for now is our salvation nearer than when we believed." Romans 13:11 (NEB & KJ)

When you travel across Canada and approach the twin cities of Port Arthur and Fort William you will notice an interesting rock formation in the middle of Thunder Bay waters. It is known as the Sleeping Giant. On the shore, the huge grain elevators witness to the tremendous economic development of Canada. By way of contrast, the Sleeping Giant rests in the bay as a symbol of the vast potential of our rich country, potential yet to be realized.

In his preface to Wallace Fisher's book, *From Tradition to Mission*, Elton Trueblood writes: "That the Church of Jesus Christ is a sleeping giant is now an accepted fact. The Church has an enormous membership and still enjoys a large measure of public respect, but it demonstrates ... only a fraction of its potential influence on our total culture."

The giant of the Church is *laity, the whole people of God*. And this giant is asleep.

I Why is the Church Asleep?

Many men and women in our Churches have gradually given up their task of witnessing and serving in the world and have delegated it to the professional minister: "Let the minister do it!" The ideal of a layman appears to be that of a pastor's helper. Furthermore, many lay people have been led to believe that service on one of the Church committees represents the fulfilment of their Christian calling.

Thus the resources of the laity are either not being used at all, or are being wasted on the marginal tasks of the Church. Instead of being dynamic witnesses to Christ in the world, the leaven of society, too many lay people are satisfied to perform mediocre duties as little Levites assisting the priest with their temple duties. The ultimate result is the self-centredness of the average local Church. We pay lip service to the top priority of missions and world evangelization. But when you examine the budgets of Canadian Churches you will discover that five to ten times as much is being spent by congregations on the maintenance of their building and organization as on the missionary task at home and abroad.

For many contemporary Christians the role of the Church is symbolized by Noah's ark. "Let the converts be gathered safely into the Church while the judgements of God fall upon a rebellious world!" The Church must offer peace and refuge in Christ. But its purpose is not exhausted by the image of Noah's ark. Too easily the Church becomes the boat of Jonah's escape, rather than the ship of Paul's missionary obedience. Like Jonah, many congregations choose a pleasure cruise instead of a witness march to Nineveh. Like Jonah, they try to sleep through the storms of our generation. But the world cries in mortal anguish: "What's the matter with you, sleeper? Get up, call on your God! Perhaps your God will think about us that we may not perish." (Jonah 1:6, Berkeley)

II How will the Sleeping Giant be Awakened?

First of all, "the atomic power of the laity" (Alan Walker) must be released. The sixteenth-century reformation set the Word of God free and made it the center of the Church life. A new reformation or awakening is needed today. It must *set the people of God free* to carry out their mission in the world rather than to carry on a routine of religious rituals in Church edifices. God bestows His charismatic gifts of the Spirit (cf. Rom. 12:4-8; I Cor. 12:8-11 & 28-31; Eph. 4:8-12; I Peter 4:10) upon every member of Christ's body, and thus makes provision for the total ministry of the whole people of God. A wise pastor will seek to discover and recognize the specific gifts of each member.

Secondly, *the laity must be prepared* for its mission in the world. The best training follows the pattern initiated by Jesus. He chose the original Twelve (1) that they should be with Him and (2) that He might send them out to proclaim the good news and to demonstrate the power of God through

I: The Sleeping Giant

acts of love and compassion (Mark 3:14-15). In other words, the training consists in the interaction of two elements: closeness to Christ and involvement in society. The missioners are plunged into the world for *action* and then retreat into their own fellowship for *reflection* and spiritual renewal. One of the best expressions of this pattern is found in small groups which are related closely to a local Church.

Last but not least, the sleeping giant will be awakened *only by the Spirit of God* in answer to a praying remnant. In his analysis of the roots and results of the Great Welsh Revival in 1904, G. Campbell Morgan wrote:

> ...A praying remnant has been agonizing before God about the state of the beloved land, and it is through prayer the answer of fire has come... If you and I could stand above Wales, looking at it, you would see fire breaking out here, and there, and yonder, and somewhere else, without any collusion or prearrangement. It is a divine visitation in which God is saying to us: "See what I can do without the things you are depending on; see what I can do in answer to a praying people; see what I can do through the simplest, who are ready to fall in line, and depend wholly and absolutely upon me." Within five weeks 20,000 have joined the Churches.

There were two characteristic marks of the awakening. (1) In every instance, there was an unusual awareness and confession of sin as people were brought much closer to the Holy God. (2) Christians were turned into evangelists. Jesus promised: "I came to send fire on the earth" (Luke 12:49a). "To be a Christian is to be part of that fire – to burn for His sake and to share in setting the world on fire" (Leslie Newbiggin).

III Why Should the Sleeping Giant be Awakened?

There are two main reasons for the awakening of the people of God. First of all, our world, in its state of decay and despair, needs a clear and powerful witness to Jesus Christ, the only hope. No Church will ever experience an awakening by the Spirit of God if it seeks renewal for its own sake (to grow in numbers or to gain prestige). God sends an awakening *for the sake of the world*, "that the world may believe" (John 17:21).

There is yet another note of extreme urgency. "Now is the high time to awake out of sleep: for now is our salvation nearer than when we believed". *Christ will come again. Will He find us asleep?* (Cf. Matthew 25:5; Mark 13:35-37; I Thess. 5:6)

"In all this, remember how critical the moment is. Now it is high time to awake out of sleep."

[Note: A Digest of the Opening Devotional Address to the Atlantic Baptist Convention Assembly at Wolfville, August 31, 1967. Reprinted from *Atlantic Baptist*, December 1, 1967, p. 2. The twin cities of Port Arthur and Fort William, mentioned in the opening sentence, have since been merged, and renamed Thunder Bay.]

J. THE STATE OF THE CONVENTION (B.C.O.Q.)

A Personal Submission to the Commission on the State of the Convention, March 21, 1968.

During the past nine years, I have visited most churches in our Convention, many of them on several occasions. I have listened to several thousands of our people, individually and in groups. On the basis of such direct contacts with our constituency, I wish to submit the following observations.

Part I Some Causes and Cures of our Present Difficulties

1. *Lack of Spiritual Vitality*

We have listened, in recent years, to many analyses of our spiritual sickness. Too many of these dealt with symptoms rather than with causes. In some respects, we are probably reaping now the final harvest of what has been sown over the past three to four decades. In other respects, our spiritual weakness is related to our culture of affluence and worship of material benefits. Lack of theological convictions, a diminishing sense of concern for the salvation of fellow human beings, and a general loss of a sense of mission and direction have been the crucial factors. During the past five years, we have aggravated the crisis by our preoccupation with organizational structures (since the 1964 reorganization) in place of a genuine concern for depth of devotion and commitment.

What are some of the cures? We must strive to avoid, at local church level and at Convention level, excessive expenditure of time and energy on matters of organization ("to keep the machine running"). In the next few years, the Convention efforts and leadership should be geared primarily to spiritual renewal rather than to organizational improvements. Here are some suggestions: regular retreats for deacons and other church leaders; days of prayer (called by the President); a network of small house groups; greater emphasis on devotional life and commitment at the Convention assembly; stress on the church as mission.

2. *Theological Divisions*

A gradual shift in leadership and initiative, from the "more liberal" to the "more conservative" position, has been taking place in our Convention over the past ten to fifteen years.

It is related, on the one hand, to the change of generations (the generation which led the Convention after the split in the 1920's tended to react to the split by taking a more "liberal" stand), and on the other hand, to the general strengthening of and a sense of solidarity among conservative evangelicals in North America (cf. the trend represented by the periodical *Christianity Today*).

It is regrettable that the "liberal" minority in our Convention has been unwilling, in most cases, to admit this general shift in our theological outlook. The New Curriculum issue was symptomatic of the more general trend. Attempts to explain the New Curriculum controversy as the result of agitation "from outside the Convention" or, of "mob hysteria", only indicate a lack of perception of the changes in the theological climate in our Convention.

Fortunately, this Convention has very few theological extremists on either left or right. The vast majority of ministers and laymen follow a course which may be described as "middle-of-the-road", with a substantial majority leaning toward a mildly conservative position. If we can ignore the few extreme voices on either left or right, and if those among us who lean more to the left of the centre will recognize the fact that the majority leans in the opposite direction, we should be able to live together in beneficial creative tension and with a common purpose. As Baptists we cannot expect credal unanimity but we can have a sense of unity in spite of

J: The State of the Convention

theological differences. Theological polarization into camps should be avoided by all means.

3. *Pressures of Ecumenicity*

In my address to the Baptist Federation of Canada triennial assembly in Ottawa last July I have attempted to describe our dilemma in terms of "social ecumenicity" and "theological ecumenicity" *[see selection F in this book]*. I cannot foresee any easy solutions in this area of conflict.

I do believe, however, that we are entering a new stage in our ecumenical relations. We must have the courage to avoid lopsided ecumenicity which finds its expression exclusively through the limited official channels provided by the Canadian Council of Churches (C.C.C.), and to seek effective and regular contacts with additional groups (presently outside the C.C.C.) with which we have more in common in terms of historical roots and concepts of church life (e.g., other Baptist groups, the Mennonites, Associated Gospel Churches). Only thus shall we be involved in real, total ecumenicity.

Part II Suggested Changes in Convention Structures

[Deleted here]

Part III The Faculty of McMaster Divinity College

There is a great need to draw the faculty into closer involvement in Convention life. Since the Convention provides a substantial part of the Divinity College budget, the Convention has a legitimate claim on the talents and time of the professors. Members of the faculty should serve as resource persons on commissions and committees, help develop Convention programs, write program booklets and provide other types of leadership. Such a service has been rendered by only a few faculty members in the past.

This is one reason why the Convention can afford to dispense with the present "program" secretaries [e.g., Christian Education]. If the faculty is to perform this important leadership function for the Convention at large, its theological outlook should reflect the general shift to "more conservative" position described earlier. Otherwise, the leadership provided by faculty members, whether in writing or in person, would hardly find the desired response among the churches, and we would face another "crisis in confidence". These observations should in no way be misunderstood as suggestions for interference with academic freedom. But a college which is as closely related to a church body and supported by itn as McMaster Divinity College is, should reflect the theological spectrum of the whole constituency.

Part IV National Baptist Leadership (Baptist Federation of Canada)

Gradually, under the guidance of God, Baptists across Canada should strive to develop two levels of secretarial leadership: (a) national secretaries for the main program areas (e.g., Evangelism, Christian Education) (b) a network of area ministers to do the field work.

Such a system would eliminate the present duplication of programs developed independently by the three conventions. It would reduce considerably the total number of secretaries and thus save thousands of dollars. It would be in keeping with present-day trends of Canadian life. The re-organization in Western Canada and the suggested changes in Ontario and Quebec would prepare the ground for such national administration.

K. BELIEVERS IN EXPECTATION (1979)

Scriptures: Acts 3:1-11; Hebrews 11:1

We have come to the countdown. We are about to launch the Baptist Federation spaceship for its journey through the next triennium. At this Assembly we have tested and re-examined many vital functions of our ship. Will all the systems work when we are in orbit, or shall we come tumbling down like the space lab? Is God really in the control tower? We have been told over and over again to expect and to demonstrate a difference in our attitudes, actions, values and lifestyles. The question that remains to be answered is this. When we look back to Regina a year from now, three years from now, ten years from now, shall we be able to say, "God met me in Regina, and it made a difference?"

At this assembly, we have given attention to the global significance of our theme and to national issues, but ultimately it all comes down to every individual person: Am I a believer with an expectant faith? Are we a fellowship of such believers? The text before us is the classical definition and affirmation of faith, found in Hebrews 11:1 (the New English Bible version): "What is faith? Faith gives substance (assurance) to our hopes, and makes us certain of realities we do not see." In the New International Version: "Faith is being sure of what we hope for, and certain of what we do not see." Let us consider the meaning of these words, first, as illustrated in the well-known incident recorded in Acts 3:1-11.

In your imagination visit with me the city of Jerusalem a short time after the day of Pentecost, the beginning of the fellowship of believers. It is a hot afternoon, just before 3 p.m. Many people are taking their daily siesta after lunch. But Peter and John, full of perspiration, are climbing up the temple hill. Why? Because it is the hour of prayer. The Living Bible paraphrases: "they are going to take part in the 3 o'clock daily prayer meeting."

Open Doors

At the so-called Beautiful Gate to the temple area they pass a beggar, a cripple from birth. Will they notice him? "The city is full of beggars. So what? We can't help them all anyway. Why doesn't the Roman government do something about it, or the wealthy temple authorities which receive gifts from the Jews all around the world? The beggar is a poor prospect for church membership anyway. What we need is a few men like Zacchaeus, converted in their heart and their pocketbook. Our young church is already looking after many poor persons and widows. Besides, we must hurry on to the prayer meeting."

Do you think something like that went through the minds of Peter and John as they noticed the beggar at the gate? Perhaps. They might have even recalled the parable of the good Samaritan, and if they were tempted to ignore the begging cripple, and hurry on to the temple, they might have thought of the Priest and the Levite (in the parable) passing by the man in the ditch. We do not know what struggle, or exchange of words, might have taken place, but we know one thing for certain. "They stopped." They made a deliberate choice of personal concern for one lame beggar, nameless to them, and without a name in the New Testament, one of the hundreds, perhaps thousands of beggars in the city.

They stop, and Peter says to the beggar: "Look at us." The beggar is surprised. Most people passing by just toss a coin, or ignore him. No one ever stops to talk to him. Phillips translates: "The man looks at them expectantly." I wonder what he is expecting. Luke, the writer of the Book of Acts, suggests that he is expecting a gift. But I wonder. He probably does not know what to expect. These men are so different from the passing crowd. What are they going to do? Here it comes. Peter says to him: "I have no silver or gold, but I will give you what I have. In the name of Jesus Christ of Nazareth, WALK." Note Peter's expectant faith. He does not say, stammeringly, the words: "In the name of Jesus Christ of Nazareth, rise." He grasps the man by his right hand and pulls him up. He expects the miracle to happen. With the eyes of

K: Believers in Expectation

faith he can already see the lame man walking, and what he anticipates in faith, happens.

The beggar catches on. He believes. His feet and ankles grow strong. He stands up. He starts to walk, and then he goes with them to the temple, and jumps around, and praises — whom? GOD. You would expect him to praise Peter and say: "Look at him, he healed me." No. He praises God. That would suggest that he has been not only physically healed but also converted to a living faith in the name by the power of which he was healed: the name of Jesus. What a fulfillment of an expectant faith! What a contrast to the failure of the same disciples to heal a young epileptic after their return from the Mount of Transfiguration!

A late medieval pope is reported to have boasted: Times have changed. The successors of Peter no longer need to say: "Silver and gold have I none." To which a cardinal remarked: "Nor can they say, as Peter did, rise up and walk." Is it not true that today most of our churches, and we as preachers and lay leaders, often resemble more the lame man at the Beautiful Gate, than the apostles? We can raise money by sophisticated methods of begging, but can we raise people from their infirmities of the body, their anxieties of the mind and above all, from spiritual death? Do we have expectant faith, the faith which "gives substance to our hopes, and makes us certain of realities we do not see yet?" Could it be that the three keys implied in the experience of Peter and John may unlock the future for us as believers in expectation?

I. The first key is **PRAYER**. Prayer is the expression and cultivation of a God-centred life. When I pray, I admit my dependence upon God. With expectant faith I claim what He promised to do for me, in me and through me. Almost a hundred years ago, the Czech philosopher and political leader, then professor in Vienna, Thomas Masaryk, undertook a thorough study of the growth of suicide rate in Europe. The conclusion of his sociological and philosophical research was this. The main reason for the spread of suicide in Europe in the closing decades of the nineteenth century was the loss of faith in God. "Man cannot live on his own," wrote Masaryk. "He either hangs on God, or he will hang on a rope."

I can bear witness to the power of prayer in my own life. As a teenage boy I was seriously ill, confined in a hospital. The doctors gave up the hope of saving my life. My parents did not. Through the night, with our pastor, they prayed believing that God could intervene. And they also pledged my saved life to His service. I know I am not my own. I have a lease on life, provided that I live for Him.

Is that not true of all of us? To me the Bible is not so much a record of sacred history, as a book of prayers and a collection of diaries of prayer-life. From Adam and Abraham to Jesus and his apostles, the people of God were marked by effective communication with God. As James expressed it: "The prayer of a righteous man has great power in its effects." Who among us could not repeat the life motto of William Carey, the pioneer Baptist missionary: "Expect great things from God and therefore, attempt great things for God."

What kept the tragically tested Adoniram Judson from going insane in Burma? His prayer hut where he withdrew three times a day to seek new power from God. When Charles H. Spurgeon was showing a group of visitors through his Tabernacle in London one Sunday before the morning service, he brought them to a door and said: "Now I will show you our heating plant." He opened the door, not to the furnace room, but to a hall where several hundred people were praying before the beginning of the service.

But we need not go overseas to see models of expectant prayer among Baptist people. At its meeting in Chester, 1837, the Baptist Association of Nova Scotia recommended to all churches to observe what they called "the monthly concert of prayer for the heathen." When Madame Feller arrived in North America to serve among French Canadians, as she travelled by coach from New York to Montreal in October 1835, she asked to be told when they reached the boundary between the United States and Canada, so that she might

K: Believers in Expectation

enter into her field of labour on her knees, literally. Her biographer remarks: "Her prayers were a power." Could it be that the spiritual hunger we are beginning to see in Quebec and among French Canadians generally in Canada today, is in part the fruit of her prayers?

The question is not what we can do for God and his kingdom, but rather to what extent we allow Him to work in us and through us. To realize this fundamental law of the Kingdom work is no less a revolution than the Copernican replacement of the geocentric view with the heliocentric view of the universe. Not the earth, but the sun is the centre. It is not what I do but what He does. Did not Jesus say: "I will build my church"? Since the true church of Jesus Christ is made up of born again believers, and since the miracle of the new birth is the work of the Holy Spirit, do we not confess that we are entirely at the mercy of God? A believers' church is always only one generation away from extinction. Furthermore, its effective ministries depend on the exercise of the gifts of the Spirit. That is why prayer is the heartbeat of the fellowship of believers. As G. Campbell Morgan expressed it: "We cannot organize revival, but we can set our sails to catch the wind from heaven when God chooses to blow upon His people once again."

II The second key to the future of the church which is made up of believers in expectation, is, focus on **PERSONS**. In contrast to other world religions and religious philosophies, many of which are now invading Canada and capturing the minds of our young people, the Christian faith is personal through and through. Our faith is not derived from a set of religious ideas or beliefs about God. It is born from, and lives by a relationship to a Person, Jesus Christ, the Son of God. Jesus said: "He who sees me, sees the Father." Furthermore, a church is healthy and growing only if it majors on personal relationships among its members and with people in the community.

The Kingdom of God grows by one person at a time. Why do we emphasize it? Because this fundamental focus on individual persons is under attack today. The contemporary society, both in the West and the East, is threatened by the demonic forces of depersonalization. We are being reduced to social insurance numbers and credit card numbers. Nobody is interested any more in our names and faces. Soon, we shall be controlled by computers. I have lived under two totalitarian regimes, Nazi and Communist. I know whereof I speak, when I call the depersonalization process demonic. Churches are in great peril when they place priorities on programs, properties and promotion instead of persons. We dare not champion the cause of human rights in other parts of the world, unless we demonstrate our concern for persons here.

If the church should fail in its struggle against the demonic forces of depersonalization, which ultimately cannot but lead to totalitarian oppression, who shall be the incarnation of Christ's concern for persons in our society? Let us get to the root of Christian personalism. Why do we as Christians insist on the supreme worth of every individual human being? Because the highest value on earth, in our view, is not success, achievement, organization, political or military power. It is the one human being, every human being, every child or adult: human beings alone have eternal destiny, and will share in the eternal life of God. Everything else will pass away: countries and nations, philosophies and universities, cultures and church buildings. You and I are the only link with eternity.

III The third key to our future is **PROPHETIC FAITH**, faith which anticipates what is not yet visible, and expects it to happen. "Faith gives assurance to our hopes and makes us certain of realities we do not see yet." The original meaning of the Hebrew word "prophet" can be translated literally "seer": a person who can see things which other people cannot see.

Good examples of such anticipatory faith are artists, composers, sculptors, painters, or architects. Any of them can see, with the eyes of his genius, the shape of his creation before he begins to chisel at the stone, or dip the brush in the paint. When Beethoven became nearly deaf towards the end of his life, he would walk through forests and parks around Vienna, and with his inner ear he could hear the tunes and

K: Believers in Expectation

harmonies of his compositions before he wrote them down. He never heard them with his physical ear.

True faith is like that. It is not merely an affirmation of doctrinal beliefs and convictions, important as that is in our generation of confusion and conflict of ideologies. Nor is it primarily an emotional excitement or "spiritual high", indispensable as that is to Christian experience. Faith is the supreme gift from God which makes it possible for you and me to expect God's interventions in life. God can intervene in any sphere of life. He can break human pride and produce repentance. He can save a broken marriage. He can influence political decisions and the destinies of nations. "I believe in God the Father Almighty, Creator — and Maintainer — of heaven and earth."

Such expectant faith has been paralysed in our generation by the tragic dichotomy between personal piety, and evangelism related to it, on the one hand, and social activism, on the other. It is a false alternative. God has never offered to the church, and to individual believers, a choice between private devotional religion, and involvement in the problems of society. Life is a whole, and Jesus Christ is Lord over all.

For us, or at least for me, the two great Baptist leaders of our generation, Billy Graham and Martin Luther King Jr., do not symbolize alternate ways of the Kingdom of God. They can be seen as prophetic spokesmen for the same Gospel, the same power of God's Spirit who can change individuals and social order. Could it be that at this time of unhealthy polarization among the churches in Canada and elsewhere, the main contribution which we as Canadian Baptists, placed in the very centre of the denominational spectrum, can make is to demonstrate the wholeness of faith and the synthesis between the personal gospel of individual salvation and the social implications of the total Lordship of Christ in society?

After his home was bombed in January 1956, Martin Luther King Jr. sought seclusion and prayed: "I have nothing left ...I can't face it alone." God met him and said to him: "Stand up for righteousness ...Stand up for truth ...and I will be on your side." In such expectant faith, he preached at the Lincoln Memorial in Washington on August 28, 1963: "I have a dream that my four little children one day will live in a nation where they will not be judged by the colour of their skin but by the content of their character... With this faith we will be able to hew out of the mountains of despair the stone of hope. With this faith we will be able to work together, to pray together, to struggle together, to go to jail together, to stand up for freedom together, knowing that we will be free one day."

Such vision and expectant faith is not a privilege for a few leaders with a special charisma. All Christians can claim the promise of Joel: "In the last days, says the Lord, I will pour out my Spirit on every one. Your sons and daughters will proclaim my message, your young men will see visions and your old men will dream dreams." Do we pray long enough so that we can dream dreams and see visions of tasks to be carried out? Are we believers in expectation?

Here are the three keys to such expectant faith: a life of prayer, focus on persons, and a prophetic vision. Take these keys and use them so that before long, we shall be able to apply the words of G. Campbell Morgan, originally written about the awakening in Wales, seventy-five years ago, to a God-sent renewal in our lives, our churches, our nation:

> If you and I could fly over Canada, you would see fire breaking out here, and there, and yonder, and somewhere else, without any collusion or prearrangement. It is a divine visitation in which God — let me say this reverently — in which God is saying to us: "See what I can do without the things you are depending on; see what I can do in answer to a praying people; see what I can do through the simplest, who are ready to fall in line, and depend wholly and absolutely upon me."

[Note: Address as President-elect to the 12th Triennial Assembly of the Baptist Federation of Canada in Regina, SK,

July 15, 1979. Reprinted from *Expect a Difference: The Report Volume of the Baptist Federation of Canada 1976-1979* (Brantford, ON, 1979), pp. 50-53.]

Open Doors

L. CAN GOD TURN THE TIDE? (1982)

Scriptures: I Kings 18:20-24 and 36-39; Psalm 119:36-40 (N.I.V.); Acts 1:6-8

I did not grow up by the sea. I was twenty-one years old when I first saw a seashore. Then, during the next decade of my life, I crossed the Atlantic Ocean by ship three times. That was enough to cure me of any enthusiasm for the sea. For twenty years I lived in Southern Ontario, far removed from the smell of salt water, and visited the Maritimes but twice.

Since 1968, my family and I learned to appreciate the symphony of the ocean waves beating their unending variations of rhythm and sound against the rocky shores of the Bay of Fundy. But I doubt whether that aesthetic, and sometimes ecstatic experience has made me any the wiser to deal with the *theological* question expressed in our topic: Can God turn the tide? — the only topic on the program of our assembly which is stated as a question.

1. Can God Turn the Tide?

What tide are we investigating? We are using the term in a symbolic way to describe major trends in the religious and moral life of our society, in our churches, our homes and our personal lives. These are the four circles of concern to which other speakers will apply the theme. I shall avoid any specific consideration of them in this general exploration of the topic.

The Baptist Federation of Canada assembly which opened on Dominion Day is an appropriate reminder that as a national body, we have, together with other Christians, responsibility to God for our land and for all the people who dwell in it. Canadian society appears to be sliding into the worst economic crisis since the 1930's.

In the longer perspective, another crisis may be even more alarming: the widespread rejection of any absolute

L: Can God Turn the Tide?

standards for human behaviour, and the implied practical atheism. In a country with a growing population, most mainline denominations are reporting not only losses in membership but also drastic decline in participation. The growth of several smaller evangelical groups should be noted but this, in itself, has been insufficient to offset the process of secularization in Canada, both French and English.

In his recent report on the second survey of religious beliefs and practices of Canadians, Professor Reginald Bibbey of the University of Lethbridge, Alberta, sums up:

Although 90% of Canadians claim to be either Protestant or Roman Catholic, less than half of them (42%) are actually church members, and less than one-third (28%) attend services on a regular weekly basis. Church attendance is highest among conservative Protestants, and lowest (about 20%) among persons with Anglican or United Church reported affiliation.

Furthermore, only about one in five Canadians give evidence of commitment to traditional central Christian beliefs, such as the divinity of Jesus and life-after-death.

The trend toward a pagan society has been accelerated by various secular ideologies which have in common three basic convictions: to dethrone God; to enthrone man in God's place; and to reject any notion of sin as transgression against God-given unchanging standards of behaviour. If sin is not faced seriously, there is no search for forgiveness and reconciliation through Jesus Christ. Life becomes a confusing and dangerous jungle. That is the road on which we march as Canadians and as members of the human race on July 1, 1982. Can the tide be turned?

That is *not* exactly the question before us. In *our* question we ask: Can God turn the tide? That is an altogether different question. If you ask, "Can the tide be turned?" your question likely reflects the agony of human doubt and despair. But if you ask, "Can God turn the tide?" your question may be understood as an affirmation of faith: I believe in a God who *can* turn the tide, *any* tide.

Open Doors

In the Old Testament, there are several examples of the tide being reversed when the people of Israel were confronted with a call to repentance and new commitment. The root meaning of the Hebrew word for repentance is in fact "to turn", to turn around, to reverse the direction, just as the waters do in the turning of the tide at sea.

When Joshua summoned the people for a large national assembly, he confronted them with a clear choice:

"If you forsake the Lord and serve idols, then he will turn against you, and do you harm, after having done you good." When the people kept shouting, "Nay, but we will serve the Lord," Joshua said to them: "Then put away the foreign gods which are among you, and *turn your heart* to the Lord, the God of Israel." And the people said: "The Lord our God we will serve, and his voice we will obey." (Joshua 24:20-24).

Many generations later, in the days of Ahab, pagan worship was so rampant that at a large rally on Mount Carmel, the prophet Elijah, as the single spokesman for the God of Israel, faced 850 prophets of the popular cults of Baal and Asherah, religions marked by ritual without change of character. The question raised by Elijah on Mount Carmel remains the key question in all movements of repentance and renewal: "How long will you sit on the fence? You cannot worship the Lord and Baal at the same time, *You must make a choice*. If the Lord is God, follow him. But if Baal, then follow *him*." (I Kings 12:21).

Several centuries later, Jesus said quietly but no less emphatically: "You cannot serve God and mammon" (Mt. 6:24) — or whatever your favourite idol or weakness of character. There is *a choice* involved in every significant turning of the tide, often a choice which is costly. More often than not, there is *a price* to be paid if the tide is to turn.

Church history records many dramatic moments when the tide was about to turn — but only at a price. A brief mention of a few names must suffice.

L: Can God Turn the Tide?

Martin Luther had to pay the price of agony and despair when he searched for assurance of salvation. Only then could he lead multitudes of his German compatriots from bondage to tradition into the glorious liberty of the sons and daughters of God.

John Wesley's heart "was strangely warmed" when God turned the tide in his life. Then, he laid all of his mental and physical energy on the altar of God, travelled to every town and village, not sparing himself—before God could turn the tide in England.

Closer to home, when God ignited the flame of new light in the soul of a young farmer from Falmouth, N.S., 200 years ago, he—Henry Alline—visited by boat, on foot or on horseback, every settlement in the Maritimes, preaching and singing the gospel of his great Redeemer. Then he collapsed of exhaustion and consumption, at the age of 36. He, and many others of our spiritual forefathers, paid the price of the Great Awakening, so that the tide could turn in the Maritimes.

With Habakkuk (3:2 TEV), we pray tonight:

"O Lord, I have heard of what you have done, and I am filled with awe. Now, do it again in our times, the great deeds you used to do."

2. Will God Turn the Tide—in 1982?

Most images which we use to illustrate spiritual truths are helpful in some respects and misleading in others. The turning of the tide is a good example of such ambiguity.

In nature, the cycle of high and low tides is as regular and predictable as day and night. You can obtain a table showing the exact times of the tides at particular Maritime locations for every day of the year. It is printed in advance. With that natural law in mind, we say: the tide turns. The fishermen make their plans accordingly, and so do the tourists who wish to see the tidal bore in Moncton.

Open Doors

The tide turns at regular intervals. But does the same law apply to spiritual life? Is the Christian church, whether local or regional, subject to a predictable cycle of low and high tides of spirituality, times of decay and seasons of renewal?

I am reminded of a church building in Toronto which I used to pass regularly when we lived in that city. Two or three times a year, a big banner would appear above the main entrance, with the words, "Revival", and beneath it, the dates, usually one week. The sign would be put up several weeks in advance, an unmistakable promise of God's intervention. Would it not be marvellous if we could, in our churches, turn on spiritual renewal like the water tap over the kitchen sink?

I do not think so. That would be tantamount to our control and manipulation of God, the way the witch doctors try to do it with their rituals. When God turns the tide, it is according to *his* calendar and *his* sovereign will. In this respect, wind may be a more appropriate symbol than the tide although the two are closely related at sea. Jesus said to Nicodemus: "The wind blows where it wills. You hear its sound, but you cannot tell where it comes from and where it is going. So it is with everyone, born of the Spirit." (John 3:8).

I believe that his words apply both to the miracle of new birth and to subsequent experiences of renewal. God controls the breezes of his Spirit but there are also conditions to be met on our side before we can benefit from his energy. A believer, and a local church, are like a sail boat. Unless you unfurl the sail and turn it the right direction, the wind may blow but it will not propel your boat.

I can find myself in the middle of an awakening in a church and yet be bypassed by God's power because I have failed to turn my own heart and conscience in the right direction. I must turn around to face God.

Such turning from self toward God is characteristic not only of the initial commitment to Jesus Christ but also of the subsequent steps of repentance in the pilgrimage of his disciples.

L: Can God Turn the Tide?

Why do some Christians seemingly fall away, while others experience renewal after a season of spiritual dryness? Why do some congregations come alive, as though a wind from heaven had blown fresh air of expectancy and zeal into every heart and home, while a neighbouring church just barely maintains routines of ritual, with no visible impact on either its shrinking flock or its spiritually-starved neighbourhood? Why have we not doubled or tripled our membership as a Federation in this generation which saw the population of Canada increase by more than ten million in the past thirty years?

Earlier I quoted data from the survey of religion in Canada by Professor Reginald Bibbey. His findings are most alarming when he reports the religious interests and involvement of school children and young adults.

At the present time, only one-third of Canadian school children are being exposed by their parents to any religious instruction and worship experience in churches. Only 15% of Canadian young adults under the age of 30 attend church regularly.

On the basis of that, I would conclude: Without a powerful movement of revival which would transform the thousands of indifferent and biblically illiterate Canadian church members — including many Baptists — into committed disciples of Jesus Christ and zealous witnesses to his redeeming power, we shall face, in this decade, the prospect of a country with fully secular culture and values, not unlike Western Europe and Great Britain.

What a vast mission field this country has become in one generation!

3. Is God Turning the Tide?

On the front cover of our program book and in *Assembly 82* promotion there is a picture of The Hopewell Rocks in Albert County, and our theme, "Turning the Tide." If you had good eyes, you noticed a little white spot at the bottom of the main rock in the centre. The dot is a person, a man or a woman, dressed in white shirt and blue jeans, walking towards the sea. For the purposes of our assembly, he (or she) may be identified as a solitary Canadian Baptist depressed over the tide which has gone out on us. That is the mood in which some of us might have arrived here.

The back cover may symbolize the conclusion of our assembly. What does it say? "A Call to Witness". I can visualize that lonely Canadian Baptist on the Bay of Fundy shore turning around, because the tide has turned. He not only walks but runs as the fresh tide drives him toward the shore where the people are. "I have good news for you," he shouts. "The tide has turned! The tide has turned!"

William G. McLoughlin, one of the best informed interpreters of the movements of revival in North American history, claims that in the 1970s the population of the United States began to pass through what he calls the Fourth Great Awakening. Among other supporting evidence he cites the rise of the Jesus People, the spread of the charismatic movement, the unprecedented growth of neo-evangelicalism (50 million persons who claim to be "born-again" Christians?) and the leadership of Jimmy Carter as the "born-again" president. There is hardly evidence as yet of any comparable trend in Canada at the present time.

Most movements of spiritual awakening in the past occurred in times of serious social and political trouble. When conditions grow desperate, many people wake up to reality and begin to search for solid answers to the quest for the meaning of life and death, to say nothing of the threat of nuclear annihilation which our generation faces. Could the present conditions in Canada, and in the world, set a stage for a major movement of spiritual awakening? Or, are we heading, as some predict, for a wave of widespread apostasy, one of the signs of the end?

The unmistakable evidence of whether the tide has turned in your life and mine during this assembly will be apparent when we return to our churches and communities across Canada. On the original Day of Pentecost, there were

L: Can God Turn the Tide?

gathered in Jerusalem about one hundred and twenty believers who were transformed by the tide of the Holy Spirit. There are at least twenty times as many of us here on Dominion Day, 1982. We look back to the first Pentecost as the birthday of the church and of its global mission. Shall we, by God's grace look back to the Moncton assembly as the turning point in your life and mine, when the Spirit of the Lord turned us from fatigue to fervour, from ignorance to enlightenment, from indifference to enthusiasm, from barrenness to fruitfulness?

The time to play at religion is over. Merely inherited religious customs, without a genuine personal commitment to Jesus Christ, will not do. For too long Canadian churches have been giving up one area of life after another. It is time to reverse the tide. It is time for an offensive. We cannot do it alone as one denomination. We must be willing to co-operate with all concerned Christians in Canada as we pray and work for renewal.

Can God turn the tide?

Will God turn the tide?

Is God turning the tide here and now?

We pray with the psalmist (Ps. 119:37, 36, 38, 40 NIV): "Turn my eyes away from worthless things.

Renew my life according to your word.

Turn my heart toward your statutes, and not toward selfish gain.

Fulfill your promise to your servant.

Renew my life in your righteousness," through Jesus Christ, your Son, our Redeemer and Lord. Amen.

[Note: Presidential address at the 13th Triennial Assembly of the Baptist Federation of Canada in Moncton, NB, July 1, 1982. Reprinted from *Turning the Tide: The Report of... The Baptist Federation of Canada—Assembly in Moncton, 1982*, pp. 24-27.]

Open Doors

Turning the Tide: A Call to Witness

The central task of the church is witness to Jesus Christ as Saviour and Lord. Without such clear and consistent witness, the church betrays its God-given purpose, and ceases to be the church (Mt. 28:18-20; John 15:16; Acts 1:8; Rom. 1:16). Witness to Christ in words and deeds is not a matter of choice or preference for a Christian. It is the inevitable result of being reborn and filled by the Spirit of God. A believers' church is built on personal profession of faith (Matthew 16:16-19) and depends on evangelism for its life and growth.

As members of the Council of the Baptist Federation of Canada, elected or appointed to represent Baptist people in our land, we affirm the commission of our Risen Lord "to make disciples", and call upon our churches across Canada to make evangelism the top priority in their congregational life and work in 1982.

With expectant faith, we look forward to the Baptist Federation of Canada Assembly in Moncton, New Brunswick, July 1-4, 1982, where, in a representative and symbolic way, we shall launch the nation-wide simultaneous thrust in evangelism. We urge every congregation to plan for an intensive program of evangelism to take place during the months of October and/or November, 1982, using the methods of outreach which are best suited to the local needs.

We, therefore, proclaim the theme of the 1982 Assembly, "Turning the Tide", as the goal of our 1982 thrust in evangelism. We pray that by the grace of God and through the obedient service of our people and of many other Christians, the tide of personal alienation from God and of secularization of society might be turned into a time of renewal, redemption and reconciliation, in the life of individuals, in homes, churches and in our nation, so "that this people may know that thou, O Lord, art God and that thou has turned their hearts back" (I Kings 18:37).

L: Can God Turn the Tide?

Dr. Jerry Zeman, President
Baptist Federation of Canada

[Note. Reprinted from the same volume as the preceding address.]

M. POTENTIAL FOR RENEWAL (1985)

The month of May marks the 40th anniversary of the end of World War II in Europe. I can well recall the sense of exhilaration which everybody in my village felt when, after six years of occupation by the German army and harassment by the secret police, Czechoslovakia was restored as an independent democratic state. We were the beneficiaries of the victory and liberation achieved by the allied powers, among them Canada.

The prisoners were set free, the survivors of concentration camps returned home, and the Czech universities, closed by the Nazis, reopened in the fall of 1945. I was among the youngest students at the old university in Prague. The campus, the city and the whole country were permeated with anticipation of a great future. We sensed a potential for renewal. Could little Czechoslovakia, we asked ourselves, serve as a bridge between the Western democratic and Eastern socialist countries, point the way to a peaceful co-existence, and thus reduce the risk of another global war? In our jubilation we could not foresee how shortlived our freedoms would be.

While a student in Prague, I travelled by train, through West Germany, to a conference in Holland. I shall never forget that journey. Standing at the window during a clear moonlit night, I looked for several hours at the deserted ruins of the great industrial cites, turned into cemeteries of civilization by the ravages of war. Like the prophet Ezekiel of old, I asked myself: Will the dead live again?

They did. The cities, including many church edifices, were rebuilt. The postwar material reconstruction in Western and Eastern Europe was impressive. But what about the renewal of the people?

1. Renewal of Society

Since I have not experienced the situation on other continents, I shall limit my observations on renewal to Europe and North America. In Western society, the material

M: Potential for Renewal

prosperity of the 1950s and 1960s did not answer the basic questions about the meaning of human existence. The protest movements of the "hippy" generation clearly demonstrated that.

Participation in the traditional forms of church life in Britain and Western Europe has declined to its lowest level. Yet a hunger for a genuine religious experience is much in evidence. But many of the seekers are bypassing the churches, and turning instead to other religions and to the occult.

Meanwhile, the Communist system in Eastern Europe also has failed to satisfy the search, by an increasing proportion of their people, for deeper meaning of life. The Marxist ideologists are puzzled by the survival, and in some places, revival of religion after a thorough—and often brutal—indoctrination of the population with atheistic philosophy for the past two generations.

Is there an explanation for this paradox? If my study of history and my pilgrimage of life in four different political and cultural contexts have taught me anything, it is this. Political ideologies and economic systems *cannot* and should not give answers to the ultimate questions of human existence. That is the function of religion and philosophy.

When a government or political party claims to provide an all-inclusive value system for its citizens, it becomes totalitarian: it seeks to control the totality of human life. Such a government must then be challenged to retreat into its legitimate and clearly delineated spheres of responsibility, namely the civic affairs, and no more. That applies to Canada as much as to any other country.

The Bible and history provide us with examples of men and women who had the courage to expose the demonic dimensions of dictatorial power and to press for its dethronement. Think of Moses as he confronts the pharaoh and demands the release of the Hebrew slaves. Picture Amos as he condemns the rich for selling the poor for a pair of shoes (2:6 and 8:6). See Luther as he challenges, at the Diet of Worms, the unholy alliance between papacy and empire.

Remember Francis of Assisi and Sister Clare, the patrons of all peaceful protesters against oppressive social systems.

Do not forget Roger Williams' confrontation with the state church system in colonial America, nor Martin Luther King's protest against racial discrimination in contemporary America. Recall Dietrich Bonhoeffer in Nazi Germany, Mahatma Gandhi in colonial India, and Alexander Solshenitzyn in Communist Russia. But above all, see Jesus as he faces Pilate, and says to the representative of the empire: "You have no power over me" (John 19:11).

All these persons shared the vision of *a renewed society*, set free from oppressive powers. But none of them were utopians, with dreams of a perfect society. Those among them, who were followers of Christ, understood very well that there is no potential for a better society unless *the people* in it have changed.

Reconstruction of economic systems and social structures will not, by itself, produce new people. But persons, transformed by the power of God, inevitably have an impact on society. Reinhold Niebuhr's early work, *Moral Man and Immoral Society* (1932) offers valuable insights into this issue.

2. Renewal of Persons

There are two basic aspects to the Christian gospel. First, its realistic assessment of human nature as fallen and sinful; and second, its claim of the potential for renewal of human nature by the power of God. Both dimensions have particular relevance for our times.

Against the confidence in human goodness, so widespread in the modern political ideologies, whether Western democratic or Eastern Marxist, we confess, with Paul, the fundamental human predicament: "All have sinned and fall short of the glory of God" (Romans 3:23). Yet in the words of the same apostle, we also affirm *the potential for personal renewal* which God makes possible through his Son, and by the power of his Holy Spirit: "If any one is in Christ, he or she is a new creature" (II Cor. 5:17). "It is no longer I who live but Christ who lives in me; and the life I now live...I live by faith in the Son of God who loved me and gave himself for me" (Gal. 2:20).

In the Christian view, any person can, by an intervention of God, receive a new nature. The experience is aptly described as the new, or second birth. However, the new nature does not replace the old one. The two co-exist in every follower of Christ, through the entire spiritual journey, "the pilgrim's progress."

3. The Role of the Church in Renewal

The limited time does not allow me to include in these reflections any elaborate comments on the role of the church in the renewal of persons and society. I suspect that much, though by no means all, of the literature on church renewal, published during the past two decades, represents attempts to shuffle the structures of church life, and to salvage an institution which has lost its leadership role in Europe a long time ago, and is losing its appeal to the younger generation in North America.

A comprehensive study of teenagers in Canada by Reginald Bibby and Donald Posterski, just released under the title *The Emerging Generation: An Inside Look at Canada's Teenagers*, clearly indicates which way the tide of institutional religion is going. By the time Canadian young people reach their early 20s, only about one in six relate to church on a regular basis. Yet the search for meaning of life and appreciation of intimate friendship and love rate far above achievement and recognition by society on the reported scale of values held by youth.1

The key to the renewal of the church is not programs but people transformed by the Holy Spirit, persons with winsome character, who reflect the presence of Christ in every walk of life.

It appears that only a major movement of revival, comparable to the Methodist thrust in England during the 18th century, or to the Great Awakening in colonial America, could reverse the trend to a secular Canadian society. The revivals of the past always rekindled evangelistic zeal and global missionary vision. They also sparked renewal of ministries.

In his famous Nottingham sermon, preached and published during the Great Awakening in 1740, Gilbert Tennent, one of the fathers of Princeton Seminary and University, warned against "the dangers of an unconverted ministry." Two years later, Jonathan Edwards pleaded: "Our people do not so much need to have their heads stored, as to have their hearts touched.2

I have often wondered whether Edwards, the first great theologian in North America, would plead for the very opposite if he lived in our days, marked by heightened emotionalism in many churches and by experience-oriented existentialism in theology. The lack of clarity and conviction in Christian beliefs may well be a major hindrance to renewal today.

4. Renewal of the Universe

One final dimension of the Christian understanding of renewal must be mentioned in closing. Christianity is firmly anchored in historical events and supremely so in the incarnation of Jesus Christ. Nonetheless, the Christian faith is not oriented to the past but rather to the future.

As Christians, we believe that history moves toward the goal of the final *cosmic renewal*. With the prophet Isaiah and with several writers in the New Testament, we anticipate "a new earth and a new heaven" (Isaiah 65:17, II Peter 3:13 and Rev. 21:1).

It is worth noting that in the Greek text of the New Testament, one of the words for renewal, literally rebirth (*palingenesia*), is used only twice — and with different meanings. In the letter to Titus (3:5), it describes the *personal* "rebirth and renewal by the Holy Spirit." In the gospel of Matthew (19:28), Jesus pictures the *cosmic* climax of history as the rebirth, or renewal of all things "when the Son of Man sits on his glorious throne." The gospel offers renewal which begins with the regeneration of *persons* but finds its completion in the regeneration of the *universe*. We dare not forget that the last book of the New Testament closes with the promise, "I am coming soon," and with the prayer, "Come, Lord Jesus" (Rev. 22:20).

In Eastern European countries, the most effective witness to Christ probably takes place today at Christian funerals. They are the only permitted open air services and are attended by a cross-section of the whole population, including Communist party members and officials. At the open grave, the equality of human beings cannot be denied, and God's offer of redemption and renewal of life is extended to all.

In the present Canadian and global context, I cannot imagine a higher calling than that of the Christian ministry, whether at home or abroad. I envy recent divinity college graduates as they stand today on the threshold of their ministry of renewal.

To be sure, such a vocation is not an idle vacation even though many people in our society think so. Rather it is a path of service marked by self-denial and sacrifice. Like Jesus, we do not expect to be served. Instead we seize every opportunity to serve, and to give ourselves to others so that they, too, may be renewed by the love of God. It is only when God's love works through you and me that the real *potential* — which means power (*potentia*) — for renewal becomes available.

Endnotes

1. Reginald W. Bibby and Donald C. Posterski, *The Emerging Generation: An Inside Look at Canada's Teenagers* (Toronto: Irwin Publishing, 1985), p. 119, *et passim*. See also Hans Mol, *Faith and Fragility* (Burlington, Ont.: Trinity Press, 1985).

2. For the text of these documents, see Alan Heimert and Perry Miller, eds. *The Great Awakening* (Indianapolis-

Open Doors

New York: The Hobbs-Merrill Co., 1967), pp. 71-99 and 278 (263-290).

[Note: The substance of an address at McMaster Divinity College Convocation, May 14, 1985. Reprinted from *The Canadian Baptist*, September 1985, pp. 4-6.]

PART FIVE:
CANADIAN BAPTIST HERITAGE AND IDENTITY

N. THE COURAGE TO BE A MINORITY (1966)

"We must obey God rather than men" (Acts 5:29).

As we set out to examine some aspects of the role and mission of Canadian Baptists in the years that lie ahead, we wish to borrow a phrase from the title of one of Paul Tillich's earlier books, *The Courage to Be* — A Minority.

I. THE ROLE OF MINORITIES

The Cult of Bigness

One of the most striking characteristics of life in North America is the cult of bigness. Year after year, the car manufacturers try to outdo each other by putting on the market bigger and more powerful automobiles. The suburbanites demand larger houses and the "cliff dwellers" in the central city move to higher and higher apartment buildings. In the countryside, small farmers are being eliminated and the future seems to belong to operators of huge farms. The little red school houses have given way to unified area schools.

Hand in hand with the cult of material bigness goes the worship of numbers and statistics. The so-called polls of public opinion claim to ascertain the will of the majority. *Vox populi vox dei*. For many individuals today the voice of the people speaks with far greater authority than the voice of God. Conformity is not a sickness that afflicts only teenagers. The children contracted the germs from their parents. When I read or hear an advertisement which says loudly, "a million people cannot be wrong," I cannot help recalling the days of Hitler in Germany. Regrettably, not only one million but many millions were wrong, tragically wrong!

Open Doors

There can be no doubt that a good deal of the popular ecumenical sentiment of this continent — and we underline the word "popular", for there is no reference here to the keen theological leaders of the ecumenical movement — represents little more than a religious version of the general worship of bigness and numbers. Because a customer finds greater satisfaction in shopping in a supermarket and shopping plaza than in five corner stores, he or she concludes that one big church would serve a community more effectively than five smaller churches. Will it serve God more faithfully? That is a question which very few people ask today.

This worship of bigness is a typically North American expression of popular ecumenicity. It does not exist, for instance, in Europe. There have been big cathedrals and ecclesiastical uniformity in most European countries for a long time. But as we all know, or ought to know, they have meant anything but spiritual vitality and dynamic influence upon society.

We can expect that the next few years will be marked by a significant regrouping of ecclesiastical forces in Canada. The first century of national life in English-speaking Canada was characterized by a relative balance of influence between four or five major Protestant communions. Baptists were numbered among them. The first decade of the second century will likely see the creation of one large Protestant national church, "The Church of Canada." From then on and for some time to come, the religious life of this country will be determined, in public opinion at least, by the partnership in power and prestige between the Protestant national church and the fast growing Roman Catholic Church. All other Protestant denominations will be reduced to small minorities.

It should be noted that the emerging new ecclesiastical situation in Canada will be radically different from the religious scene in both the United States and in Great Britain. This means that in our quest for the Baptist mission in Canada we cannot simply draw parallels from their situations, nor follow their patterns and solutions, and this in spite of our friendly ties with Baptists in both lands. In the Old Country, there is a long tradition of close cooperation between all free churches banded together in their protest against the established church. The role of the Roman Catholic Church has been minimal. In the United States, the coming Protestant mergers will not, in the foreseeable future, disturb to any considerable extent the balance in relative strength between the Roman Catholic Church, and United Protestant Church (whatever name it chooses to use) and other large Protestant bodies such as the several Baptist Conventions which are not involved, at the present time, in the merger plans.

The role and the positive contribution of any religious group can be defined only within the framework of its contemporary society. We cannot discern the Baptist mission in Canada unless we understand the context of the religious life in this country. Would it be unwise to suggest that with the changing ecclesiastical scene, the role of Canadian Baptists will change as well? Is it not obvious that with the emergence of a national Protestant church, Canadian Baptists would no longer — unless they become a party in the merger — be regarded as one of the major Protestant communions in Canada but rather as a small minority? This is why it is imperative that we explore the role and mission of a minority.

Two Kinds of Minorities

There are two kinds of religious minorities. There are those which represent nothing more than petrified left-overs from the past. One may call them "conservative" or "reactionary" minorities. They try to preserve past forms, and react against new developments. The example of the Roman Emperor Julian, known as "the Apostate", serves as a case in point. In the midst of the triumphant conquest of the ancient world by the Christian Church, he tried to restore traditional paganism. Such and similar nostalgic attempts to revive the past are condemned to failure. The efforts of a group of Spanish and other cardinals at the Second Vatican Council to frustrate the proclamation of the decree on religious liberty can be cited as an illustration from the current scene.

Open Doors

Not all religious minorities, however, have their faces turned backward. In the history of Christianity, minority movements have often outdone the majority church in their creative contribution to the Kingdom of God. Minorities have served as the "avantgarde" of the future. A few examples will demonstrate the thesis.

A year ago, I stood on the bank of the river Rhine, just outside the old walls of the city of Constance on the border of Germany and Switzerland. A stone marks the place where 550 years ago, John Hus was burnt at the stake. He had the courage to oppose, with the support of only a handful of Czech followers, the claims of the Medieval Church to exercise unlimited control over the conscience and life of all people. Against the power of the Church, its council and its pope, he appealed directly to Christ and to His Word in the Scriptures. His death marked the birth of the Protestant Reformation. The little Hussite minority, ridiculed, condemned and persecuted by its contemporaries, was the vanguard of the future.

A century later, at the Diet of Worms, a humble monk faced the Emperor and the assembled representatives of political power in Germany. After a night spent in prayer, he solemnly declared that his conscience was captive to the Word of God and that unless he were convinced by Scripture and plain reason, he could not accept the authority of popes and councils. "Here I stand, I cannot do otherwise," said Martin Luther.

During the past year, as I walked the narrow streets in the old city of Zurich, I often passed one of the rich burgher houses in which the first recorded baptism of believers during the Reformation era took place on a cold January night in 1525. In the nearby village of Zollikon, a group of farmers met in homes, read the Bible, experienced radical repentance, and then bore witness to the work of God's grace in their lives, as they were baptized in homes or at the village fountain. They longed for the restitution of the kind of church about which they read in the New Testament. With all his learning, the reformer Zwingli could not refute their arguments against a national church to which every citizen belonged. Said Jacob Hottinger, "It is not given to any government — political or ecclesiastical — to dispose over God's Word with worldly means of force; is not the Word of God free?"

Many other examples of what we might call "progressive" minorities could be added from the annals of history and from the contemporary scene, to say nothing of the countless illustrations that could be cited from the Bible. We must mention at least the courageous struggle of the "Confessing Church" (*Bekenntniskirche*), a minority movement which opposed the diluted message and compromising attitudes of the German national Protestant Church during the Nazi era.

The crucial question is: How can one distinguish a "conservative" minority from a "progressive" minority? What is it that makes a minority a tool in God's hands for the accomplishment of His purposes? If the source of our witness is Baptist tradition then we are oriented towards the past and are, in fact, obeying men rather than God. The secret of a dynamic minority which bears relevant witness in its own day and for the days ahead is the courage to obey God rather than men. A "reactionary" minority follows men. A "progressive" minority obeys God rather than men.

II. The Courage to Obey God

[Deleted here].

III. The Courage to be a Minority

The President and the officers elected at this Assembly will have the distinct honor of leading the people of this Convention into Canada's Centennial Year. In the forthcoming months, Canadians will be engaged not only in solemn and gay celebrations but also in a sobering process of heartsearching. Not too many of us know why we are Canadians and what it means to be a Canadian.

There are Canadians by necessity, people like the Eskimos who have never dreamt of being anything else. There are Canadians by continuity, people who continue to live in this country because of convenience, of tradition or lack of courage to try something new elsewhere. But there are also Canadians by conviction. The last group involves both native citizens and those who have made this land their new homeland.

There is a parallel between being a Canadian by conviction and being a Baptist by conviction if for no other reason than because of the fact that Canadians as a nation are bound to remain a small ten percent minority on this continent, just as Baptists will hardly outgrow their minority status in the Canada of tomorrow. We have an admiration for families which claim Baptist descent, so to say, for several generations. But is it not true that in a real sense there are no other Baptists except those by conviction?

We have no fear that the Baptistic witness would be silenced in this country. As long as the Bible is read and its message is proclaimed there will be people who will make a Baptistic pilgrimage such as many of us did when we joined the churches of this Convention. Our concern is not for the future of Baptistic witness in Canada. Rather it is the question whether this Convention, its constituent churches, its ministers, its lay people, all of us have the courage to be a Baptistic minority and to pay the price for it, or whether we shall gradually give up our mission and leave it to others whom God would undoubtedly raise.

In pointing out this choice which confronts us, we are not suggesting, not even by implication, that a minority has a monopoly on truth, nor that we should cease to cooperate with other communions. It takes courage to be a minority. But it often takes even greater courage to cooperate with people of different convictions. Nevertheless, it is not true that what is at stake today is the issue of two divergent concepts of faith and of church? Faith can mean either an honest surrender of life to God and a personal union with Jesus Christ, or it can be little more than a nominal attachment to a religious organization. Similarly, the Church can be either a fellowship of committed disciples of Christ, or a society of people with some vague religious interests.

N: To Be a Minority

In the long history of the Church, these two concepts have never been reconciled even though many attempts for a synthesis have been made and are being made again in our generation. At times, the powerful national churches tried to suppress the more radical movements. At other times and in other places, the Baptistic groups grew so fast that they became a majority church in a given area with great risks to their spiritual vitality. But with such few exceptions, Baptist churches constitute a minority within the Church of Christ. *Do we have the courage to be a minority?*

[NOTE: Commissioning address given at the Convention [B.C.O.Q.] assembly in Hamilton, ON, on June 13, 1966. Reprinted from *The Canadian Baptist*, July 1, 1966, pp. 9, 12 and 15.]

O. THE PARADOX OF BAPTIST ORIGINS AND DESTINY (1970)

1. The Polarization of "Church" and "Sect" in Christianity.

Two opposite trends can be discerned in the history of Christianity: the one toward ecclesiastical institutionalism ("churchianity") and the other toward sectarianism. Ernest Troeltsch introduced a threefold typology of church, sect and spiritualism. In his book, *The Misunderstanding of the Church*, Emil Brunner distinguished between the *EKKLESIA* as fellowship of believers, and the institutional(ized) church. One might point out the contrast between a believers' church and a "national church", *Volkskirche*, a church to which most citizens belong and which represents some degree of Christian culture establishment in, and accommodation to a given society.

2. The Sect - Church Cycle.

Some Protestant denominations began as established churches (e.g., Lutheran, Anglican, Presbyterian). Others were originally "sectarian" movements of dissent but subsequently acquire the typical "church" characteristics, approximate the "mother church" and rejoin it. Cf. the Methodists and the Congregationalists who are in the process of completing the cycle.

3. The Paradox of Baptist History and Destiny.

The English-speaking Baptists of the sixteenth century had twofold roots: Puritan Separatism and Anabaptism. A tension between the more "churchy" and the more "sectarian" types has existed in the Baptist movement from the beginning and is still with us. Examples can be found in the diverse attitudes to the Bible, to higher education, to forms of worship, to issues of ethics, and to the role of the church in society. As

O: Baptist Origins and Destiny

though to reinforce this paradox, Baptists in Nova Scotia can trace their origins similarly to two different cradles: the tradition of an established church represented by the Congregationalist immigrants from New England, and by a group of former Anglicans in Halifax, over against the quasi-sectarian heritage of revivalism, from Henry Alline to the present.

For some reason Baptists have never succumbed to the pull toward "establishmentarian" Christianity. Both in England and in North America, they experienced several movements of revival. A steady influx of "converts" to the Baptist position has helped to keep alive the awareness of Baptist distinctives. The tension between the "church" and "sect" patterns of Christianity has sometimes resulted in denominational divisions and splits. When properly understood and held in creative tension this paradox may yet prove to be our most important contribution to the life and mission of the whole Church of Jesus Christ in our ecumenical age.

[Note. Part of a discussion paper presented at the Wolfville Baptist Church, Wolfville, NS, November 15, 1970.]

P. AUTHORITY AND FREEDOM: A BAPTIST VIEW (1970)

This brief popular article has been prepared at the request of the Editor. I wish to make it clear that I am writing merely as one member of our large Atlantic Baptist fellowship and presenting my personal convictions and observations. I am not submitting a theological essay, nor a position paper on behalf of a committee or an institution. Nevertheless, I consider myself to stand in the mainstream of the Baptist tradition.

The Power of the Word of God.

I am grateful for the opportunity to bear, first of all, my personal witness to the power of the Word of God. As a teenager in my native country of Czechoslovakia, I experienced the wonder of new birth through the reading of the Bible (cf. I Peter 1:23-25).

Since that initial impact, the regular study of the Scriptures has shaped my life and spiritual pilgrimage more than any other influence.

After an intensive search of the Scriptures, I was led, as a Presbyterian, to embrace "Baptistic" convictions with regard to baptism and the nature of the Church. Through the years of my theological studies I have always endeavoured to test my teachers and textbooks by the biblical norm. As pastor and, later as a denominational secretary, I have sought, honestly though not always effectively, to evaluate and shape all decisions and activities in the light of Scriptures. As a Church historian, I am persuaded that in the human perspective, the Church would have disintegrated at many points of its history under the pressure of syncretistic and pagan trends had it not been for the authority of the Scriptures set above the Church as the supreme rule (canon) of doctrine and practice in the early centuries of its development. In our syncretistic age, we need clear biblical preaching and teaching.

P: Authority and Freedom

Since my conversion, I have never found it difficult or perplexing to accept the authority of the Bible as the Word of God. No doubt, this is due mainly to my positive experiences of the life-transforming power of Christ through the Scriptures, both in my own life and in the lives of my friends (cf. John 7:17 and Rom. 10:17). In my theological reflection, I have learnt to view the Bible in terms of an analogy to the classical Christian interpretation of the person of Christ, namely His two natures, human and divine.

There are convincing arguments for the authority of the Bible, especially the New Testament, based on the "apostolic origin" of the writings. However, this is only one aspect, the "human", of biblical authority. The divine nature of Christ was (and still is) discernible only by faith and cannot be proved or disproved by historical arguments. Similarly, the claims for the divine origin (inspiration) of the Scriptures are either accepted by faith, or rejected because of lack of faith. I trust the New Testament (and the whole Bible) as the Word of God not merely because of its unique historical origins related to the once-for-all-ness of the historical Jesus and His apostles but also, and primarily so, because I accept — and this only by faith — the inspired origin of the biblical writings.

Inevitably, an element of mystery remains in our understanding of the Scriptures as much as in our understanding of Jesus Christ. Very few Christians (even pastors!) can explain the relationship between the two natures of Christ in precise terms such as the definitions of the Council of Chalcedon (451). Does that disqualify them from a saving faith in Jesus Christ? Similarly, are precise definitions of the inspiration of the Scriptures necessary for a genuine faith in the Bible as the Word of God?

The Lordship of Christ and "Soul Liberty"

There can be no Christianity without a Christ-centered affirmation of faith. All generations of Christians confessed Jesus Christ as the Lord. Most movements of reform and revival in the history of the Church sprang from a fresh vision of the unique Lordship of Christ over individuals, over

Church and over society. In this simple affirmation all Christians have been united. The divisions arose and still arise when one asks the crucial question: How does Christ exercise His supreme authority?

The great majority of Christendom has taught, and still claims, that the Lordship of Christ (and all His benefits) must be mediated by and through the Church. The interpretation of this "mediation" may vary from the massive hierarchical and sacramental system of Roman Catholicism to the more subtle mediation through "the ministry of Word and sacraments" in the Reformed traditions. Nevertheless, in all these traditions *the Church is placed between man and God.*

Over against such interpretations of the Lordship of Christ the Baptists have insisted on *the direct access of the individual man (soul) to God.* The leading Southern Baptist theologian, E. Y. Mullins, expressed the Baptist genius in the following capsule form: "The sufficient statement of the historical significance of the Baptists is this: the competency of the soul in religion." At the B.W.A. Congress in London (1955) another well-known spokesman for Baptists of North America, Walter P. Binns, stated:

> Baptists are agreed upon the fundamental doctrine of the competency of the individual soul to deal directly with God without the intervention of parent, priest or sacrament...From this doctrine of the competency of the individual soul comes our belief in the autonomy of the Church and the democracy of believers within the Church... Inherent in the same basic doctrine is our belief in the right of the individual to interpret the Scriptures for himself under the guidance of the Holy Spirit.

A similar note was sounded by Canadian Baptists in 1906 when the Committee on Church Union of the Baptist Convention of Ontario and Quebec in its reply to an invitation from the Presbyterian, Methodist and Congregational Church committees on proposed Union of Protestant Bodies in Canada stated:

> The Baptist belief in the immediacy of each man's relations with God and in the necessity of personal faith in Christ in order to receive salvation carries with it the universal priesthood of believers and the rejection of all forms of church policy which admit the spiritual distinction of clergy and laity, or the subjection of the individual Christian to any spiritual authority but Christ Himself.

Admittedly, such strong pleas for "the competency of the individual soul" represent extreme religious individualism which in North America has been molded to a considerable extent by the philosophy of the Enlightenment as well as by the one-sided interest of the Revival movements in the conversion of the individual, to the neglect of the life of the Church. Nonetheless, the concern for the right of every person to approach God directly, both in the search for truth in the study of the Scriptures, and in the quest for the assurance of salvation, has been one of the main emphases of the Baptist tradition from its inception in England in the early seventeenth century.

Firmness and Flexibility: Biblical Authority and Freedom of Interpretation

In his widely circulated book, *What Baptists Stand For*, Henry Cook characterized the Baptist position as being "at once firm and flexible: firm, because grounded in New Testament revelation; and flexible, because free from the rigidities of any particular theological or ecclesiastical system, and capable therefore of adaption to widely varying conditions."

To my mind, the genius of the Baptist movement can best be expressed by the diagram of an ellipse. The two foci of the ellipse are biblical authority and freedom of interpretation. The two must go together and in fact are "held together" by the central concept of the Lordship of Christ.

Open Doors

Christ can be known through the Scriptures alone. What do we know about Jesus Christ apart from the biblical records? Nothing at all. There are no other primary sources. The only way to come to know Jesus Christ, to be certain of one's salvation and eternal destiny, is to trust and accept the invitations and promises of Christ recorded in the New Testament. If you set aside the Bible, there are only two other ways left for your religious quest: your own ideas about God (religious subjectivism) or submission to the teaching and sacramental authority of the Church.

Since the Christian way is described in the New Testament as a profoundly personal experience (but not exclusively individualistic!) Baptists have always championed the right of every person to interpret the Scriptures for himself, under the guidance and illumination of the Holy Spirit. Two aspects of this "Baptist freedom" cannot be stressed enough.

It is not unlimited freedom to believe anything. It is freedom circumscribed by the authority of the Scriptures. It is merely freedom of interpretation. Otherwise we would be advocating a chaos of conflicting individual opinions which in turn would make the fellowship of the Church impossible. To quote R. F. Aldwinckle:

> Let us take two affirmations which have been integral to our Baptist witness from the seventeenth century to the present, the inspiration and authority of the Bible, and the confession of the Lordship, or if you prefer, the divinity of Christ. It seems to me that any man who denies these two affirmations, with a full awareness of what he is doing, not only ceases to be a Baptist but also a Christian.[1]

The second important modification of the "Baptist freedom" is the awareness that a wholesome interpretation of the Scriptures can never be the product of mere human reflection and knowledge of historical and literary background. In order to experience the power of the Word of God, one will not discard historical and literary data supplied by scholarly study but will seek, furthermore, *"the inward illumination of the Spirit of God."* To quote one of the most important Baptist statements, the Second London Confession of 1688 (adopted in America with minor additions as the Philadelphia Confession in 1742):

> ...our full persuasion and assurance of the infallible truth, and divine authority thereof, is from the inward work of the Holy Spirit, bearing witness by and with the Word in our hearts.... We acknowledge the inward illumination of the Spirit of God to be necessary for the saving understanding of such things as are revealed in the Word.... The infallible rule of interpretation of Scripture is Scripture itself: And therefore when there is a question about the true and full sense of any Scripture (which is not manifold but one) it must be searched by other places, that speak more clearly.[2]

The Bible and the Creeds

Through the three and a half centuries of their history, Baptists did not find it easy to maintain a balance in their "bifocal" emphasis on biblical authority and freedom of interpretation. Quite often, their ranks became polarized into two extreme camps. Some would overemphasize individual freedom to such an extent that the scriptural criteria were no longer respected. This in turn would produce a reaction in the opposite direction. Those who were concerned for obedience of biblical standards would set up doctrinal statements which presumably expressed the core of biblical revelation. They would then, in the name of scriptural authority, demand agreement with such credal statements.

Both trends, the libertine and the credalistic, violate the Baptist insights into the nature of faith and of Christ's authority. In contrast to some other denominations which equate faith with an assent to a set of doctrines ("beliefs") Baptists interpret saving faith as a personal relationship to Jesus Christ which begins in the experience of new birth and continues in growth toward spiritual maturity. The Lordship of Christ and the direct access of the individual to God through Christ apply not only to issues of truth (discussed earlier) but also to personal salvation. To demand an agreement with certain doctrines *as a condition of salvation* would remove us far from the apostolic norm recorded in the New Testament.

> Baptists neither advocate credal subscription, i.e. the binding authority of one man's or one group of men's interpretation of Scripture, nor do they advocate total theological freedom which involves freedom to deny the authority of Scripture or the Lordship of Christ. Baptists are thus called upon to tread the middle course between credal uniformity imposed by ecclesiastical tyranny and a theological openness which may result in sheer anarchy in matters of belief.[3]

The problem with creeds and confessions is that they tend to "strait-jacket" the Word of God in categories of thought which of necessity reflect only a sector of Christianity at a particular time in history. In His infinite wisdom, God provided us in the Bible with a pluralistic witness to Christ. Without any theological training, a regular student of the Bible will soon notice the differences in language and general approach between the Gospel of John and that of Mark, or between the letters of Paul, Peter and James. Most of us have our favourite books or passages of the Bible which God used to draw us to Christ and to make us grow in Him. There are many paths in the Bible and all of them lead to Christ. Thanks be to God for the inexhaustible richness of His revelation!

By contrast, most creeds or confessions are much narrower in their definitions and usually present a somewhat lopsided summary of Christian teachings. Any collection of Baptist confessions will prove this point. You will find confessions with a Calvinistic bias, others with an Arminian base. Most twentieth-century statements mirror the liberal-fundamentalist controversy.

P: Authority and Freedom

In the nineteenth and twentieth centuries, many confessions were formulated to express consensus of new bodies which came into being through mergers. A good example of such a confessional statement if *The Basis of Union of 1906* prepared as a basis for the fellowship of our Convention.[4] In the last century, most Baptist associations in our provinces had their own confessions. Many local Churches have a statement which presents, in a concise summary, the main Baptist distinctives to inquirers and prospective members. Personally, I am not opposed to such affirmations of our beliefs as long as they are kept in their rightful place as testimonies and declarations.

The All-Sufficiency of the Scriptures: "The Bible Alone" vs. "The Bible Plus"

We must reiterate that no such Baptist affirmations of faith have every acquired an authoritative value comparable to that of the Augsburg Confession for the Lutherans, the Thirty-Nine Articles for the Anglicans, or the Westminster Confession for the Presbyterians.

Among the major streams of Protestantism, Baptists have been the only consistent Protestants. They have retained the original principle of authority enunciated by the young Reformers, *Sola Scriptura*, the Scriptures alone. One might even suggest that in view of their affirmation of the all-sufficiency of the Bible Baptists have been, from the beginning of their movement, the truly "ecumenical" Christians. They added no other authority to the one foundation common to all Christians. The Bible unites, creeds and confessions divide.

When the old Christian Church agreed upon a canon of Old and New Testament Scriptures it intended to set up, once and for all, a norm of doctrine to which the Church should be subject. In subsequent centuries, the Church repeatedly betrayed its original decision and placed some other authority alongside with, or even above the Scriptures.

One of the latest examples of this trend are the tentatively approved "Principles of Union" between the Anglican and United Churches of Canada. A threefold authority is envisaged for the merged Church: (1) the Scriptures, (2) the ecumenical creeds of the ancient Church and (3) "Articles of doctrine and forms of common worship which have been authorized in our separate Churches and used by God as means of grace."

We would venture a prediction that in the remaining three decades of this century the most crucial issue in Protestantism will be the problem of authority in the Church. Will it be Scriptures alone, or the Bible plus—confessions, decrees of councils, tradition?

As Baptists, we have resisted, for the most part successfully, the temptation to elevate any human criteria to a level of authority which rightfully belongs only to the Scriptures. Our position is founded in an unwavering confidence in the power of the Word of God. Implicit in it is faith in the Holy Spirit who will guide individual believers and whole Churches in their interpretation of the Bible, and thus lead, in spite of our human limitations in understanding and our excesses in freedom, to unity in Christ.

Endnotes

1. R. F. Aldwinckle in *The Canadian Baptist*, Feb. 15, 1969, p. 16.
2. W. L. Lumpkin, ed. *Baptist Confessions of Faith* (Philadelphia, 1959), p. 250.
3. R. F. Aldwinckle in *The Canadian Baptist*, Feb. 15, 1969, p. 23.
4. Cf. the study guide on *The Basis of Union* by Harry A. Renfree (Saint John, NB, 1965).

[Note. Reprinted from *The Atlantic Baptist*, January 15, 1970, pp. 1 and 13.]

Q. BUILDING A FUTURE ON THE PAST: THE ROLE OF HISTORIANS (1990)

Historians who are committed Christians, are among the church leaders who must assume a major responsibility during any time (KAIROS) of reorientation to a different future. They should understand best the dialectic of continuity and discontinuity in the dynamic movement of history. Such a call to leadership extends to Christian historians serving in any context: to professional academics in church-related or secular institutions, as well as to lay persons who do research as a labour of love. The erection of a few guideposts may be in order on this occasion.

1. The renaissance of Baptist historical studies in Canada in the 1980s has made available many valuable resources, among them two basic tools: the first bibliography, and the first comprehensive review of "The Baptist Story in Canada" by Harry A. Renfree.[1] In both books, nearly all streams of the diverse Baptist tradition had been included, even if not always in a satisfactory manner.

There are no limits to the opportunities for research in this field of studies: from oral history projects in which any volunteer can help, to doctoral dissertations and advanced research projects not only in history and theology but also in related disciplines, such as literature and social studies. Comparative studies of Baptist and other denominational traditions are long overdue. Since opportunities for professional careers in Baptist history are very limited, persons trained in other fields had in the past, and hopefully will have in the future, a substantial share in Baptist research. Graduate students should be encouraged to specialize in Baptist studies.

2. One of the specific tasks is the preparation of a book of sources representative of all Baptist groups in Canada. That opportunity, likely for a team of historians, was made even more urgent by the recent publication of the *Sourcebook*

Open Doors

for Baptist Heritage prepared by H. Leon McBeth.[2] In vain does the reader search through the 639 pages of the otherwise remarkable book for any text from, or even a mention of, Canada. We need a source book for Canadian Baptist heritage, a selection of texts which would reflect the regional, ethnic, cultural and other differences, and yet document the fundamental unity of Baptist witness in Canada. Such a volume will not affect the continuing process of editing and publishing specific sources and other materials. The experimental project of the series "Baptist Heritage in Atlantic Canada" has demonstrated that it can be done with very modest resources.

3. Bibliographies, sourcebooks and textbooks serve as incentives to further scholarly research and popular studies. But they are also indispensable tools for teaching courses in Baptist heritage. Baptists of all shades and colours have made sacrificial investment in higher education for several generations. At the present time they sponsor the Atlantic Baptist College (liberal arts) in Moncton, New Brunswick; and ten English-speaking, as well as two French, seminaries: five in Western Canada, four in Ontario, two in Quebec and one in Atlantic Canada. There are also lay leadership training schools in Alberta and Ontario. Presumably, courses on Baptist heritage and distinctive beliefs are offered at each of these institutions.

Furthermore, several hundred Baptist students are enrolled in non-denominational seminaries in cities like Toronto, Winnipeg and Vancouver, and in many Bible Colleges, especially in Western Canada. All of these future Baptist leaders, whether lay persons or ordained ministers, should be familiar with the Baptist heritage. Without such awareness, the identity of many Baptist churches will be in jeopardy.

On the practical side, the potential sales of books to Baptist students in all these institutions, year after year, would provide a stable market for publications dealing with the Baptist heritage. Who will establish a network of the necessary personal contacts in order to promote the programs of Baptist studies?

Q: The Role of Historians

4. There are at least 2,000 Baptist congregations in Canada. How many of them celebrate the Baptist heritage in words, music, drama and displays? Do they observe anniversaries, or Heritage Sundays? Do they conduct membership preparation classes on Baptist heritage and distinctives? Baptist conferences (conventions, unions, fellowship) hold annual assemblies. Are issues of Baptist heritage and identity included in the program? Who will produce videos with popular discussions, or dramatic presentations of Baptist heritage topics?

5. Does the general population in any given area have opportunities to hear or watch informative programs about Baptists on radio and television, or read reliable releases about Baptists in the secular press?

All the research into Baptist heritage and identity represents little more than academic or antiquarian interests unless the results are channelled into courses at schools, preaching and teaching in the churches, and into public media.

6. Research and its utilization in publications require financial resources. It was a deliberate strategy of John Mockett Cramp when in his lecture on "The Future of the Baptists" at Acadia College[3] in 1852, he combined a lively interpretation of the past with a vision for the future and an appeal for an endowment fund. He understood the realities of life. If today the various Baptist archives and projects in Baptist heritage could depend more on designated capital funds than on the mercies of denominational charity, we could anticipate the future of Canadian Baptist studies with greater assurance. Without such stable support, many visions will remain dreams, recorded or forgotten.

7. Another major hindrance to the pursuit of the objectives just outlined has been the lack of cooperation among the several Baptist bodies, and their educational institutions, in Canada. Do we have the faith to expect a change during this decade?

Open Doors

The annual pastors' conferences at Banff bring together the ministers from the Baptist Union of Western Canada and the North American Baptist Conference. The Fellowship Baptists and the General Conference Baptists now cooperate in the new evangelical seminary, ACTS, on the campus of Trinity Western University. Last December, the chief executive officers of the five major Baptist bodies in Canada met for a consultation in Toronto, and agreed to meet on an annual basis in the future. The Baptist Heritage Conference in Edmonton involved participants from nearly all larger Baptist bodies in Canada.

Are these unmistakable signs of a spring thaw in inter-Baptist relations in our land? Is it premature to propose the formation of one Canadian Baptist Historical Society, with members recruited from all Baptist bodies, and open to any other persons interested in the Baptist heritage? Could one of the Baptist educational institutions sponsor and support a Centre, or Institute, of Canadian Baptist Studies?

David Priestley made a realistic assessment of the current situation when he wrote (1988): "Admittedly, some would keep old antagonisms alive, maintaining old positions with the old intransigence and belligerence; but there is a greater theological and attitudinal unity among Baptists in Canada than their organizational diversity and its roots would suggest."[4]

Baptist historians can make a contribution to the courtship and cooperation among Baptists in such projects as: co-operative ventures in publications; exchange of students and faculty members; joint celebrations of Baptist heritage in which congregations of different Baptist affiliations can see the whole rather than the fractured picture of the Baptist witness in an area.

It is time to face the understandable but unacceptable contradiction in Baptist inter-church relations. For most of this century, Baptists in the various conventions and conferences, have found it easier to relate to non-Baptist denominations, whether in the so-called mainline ecumenical or in the

Q: The Role of Historians

evangelical camps, than to build bridges of understanding and trust within the Baptist family. The same paradox applies to Baptist congregations ignoring one another in the same community.

Many factors have contributed to this fractured family tragedy. One of them which must be of concern to us, is the role which some historians played in the process of alienation. Instead of an impartial examination and evaluation of past events, they distorted equally the heritage of their particular group by hagiographic or apologetic aggrandizement, and the history of others by partial evidence, ascription of false motives, or total omission.

The time has come for a well-informed and integrated approach to Baptist historiography in Canada. Historians have a role to play in building a *better* future on the past. For generations, Baptists have affirmed — and still do today — that tradition is not an authoritative norm of faith and practice, alongside the Bible. A better understanding of their history will help Baptists overcome the ever present temptation of an uncritical acceptance of many traditional teachings and customs for which there is no basis in the Scriptures. Therefore, for more than one reason, historians have an important role to play in building a future on the past.

Endnotes

1. Harry A. Renfree, *Heritage and Horizon: The Baptist Story in Canada* (Mississauga, Ont.: Canadian Baptist Federation, 1988). Cf. also D. G. Bell, "All Things New: The Transformation of Maritime Baptist Historiography", *Nova Scotia Historical Review*, Vol. 4, No. 2 (1984): 69-81.

2. H. Leon McBeth, *A Sourcebook for Baptist Heritage* (Nashville: Broadman Press, 1990).

3. J. M. Cramp, *The Future of the Baptists and Their Duty to Prepare for It: A Lecture Delivered at Wolfville, N.S., March 25th, 1852* (Halifax, N.S.: n.d.).

4. David T. Priestley, "Canadian Baptists in National Perspective: A Narrative", *The Baptist Quarterly*, Vol. 32, No. 7 (July 1988): 321. Cf. Samuel J. Mikolaski, "Identity and Mission", in *Baptists in Canada: Search for Identity Amidst Diversity*, ed. Jarold K. Zeman (Burlington, Ont.: G. R. Welch, 1980), pp. 1-19.

[Note. Concluding part of the keynote address, "Building a Future on the Past", presented at the Baptist Heritage Conference in Edmonton, AB on May 19, 1990. Reprinted from *McMaster Journal of Theology*. Vol. 1, No. 2 (Fall 1990): 64-67.]

PART SIX:

CANADIAN BAPTISTS IN THE WIDER ECUMENICAL CONTEXT

Introductory Note (1991)

In the early 1960s, the "Baptist Jubilee Advance" (B.J.A.) five-year program (1959-1964) of cooperation with other Baptist bodies in North America in major areas of church work (Christian Education, Evangelism, Church Extension, Stewardship and World Missions) provided the initial impetus for greater consciousness of Baptist identity. The controversy over the New Sunday School Curriculum (1965) led to the severance of strong links with the United Church of Canada, and to a search for broader ecumenical contacts. The Conferences on the Believers' Church in Louisville, KY (1967) and in Winnipeg (1978) provided a crucial impetus for the process of reorientation in Canadian Baptist inter-church relations. As a national body, representing a consensus of its four constituent conventions/unions, the Baptist Federation of Canada found it necessary to terminate its membership in the Canadian Council of Churches in 1980 since the Atlantic Convention and the French Union earlier had withdrawn their support of such membership. While the Baptist Convention of Ontario and Quebec was readmitted to the C.C.C. in 1981, the Baptist Union of Western Canada joined the Evangelical Fellowship of Canada in the mid-1980s. The United Baptist Convention of the Atlantic Provinces defeated, in 1988, a private motion to join the Evangelical Fellowship of Canada. The selections which follow express personal reflections on the long and difficult search for a new Canadian Baptist identity in the ecumenical context.

Open Doors

R. THE BELIEVERS' CHURCH: WHO IS A BELIEVER? (1967)

[An abbreviated text of a response to a paper on "A Believing People: Theological Interpretation" by Warren F. Groff, presented at the Conference on the Concept of the Believers' Church in Louisville, KY, 1967]

In response to Dr. Groff's paper and in preparation for our discussion I wish to raise several questions. Because of the limitations of time, my observations will be focused exclusively on the term "believing" (people).

1. What is *the difference* between congregations which claim to be believers' churches and those which admit "mixed membership"?

In a recent statement on *Church Membership* released by the United Church of Canada, reference is made to two basic concepts of church membership: a "broad and inclusive" concept of the established churches of Europe where citizenship and church membership were nearly synonymous (*corpus Christianum*) and a "narrow and exclusive" concept which stresses a personal decision to accept Christ as Saviour and Lord as the prerequisite of church membership. According to the statement, the United Church of Canada "stands at neither of these extremes but like most of the larger Protestant Churches it follows *a middle way* in this manner... It makes little attempt to lay down minimum standards of religious attainment, or to discriminate between 'true believer' and 'nominal Christian'.... The Church, like the children of Israel, is a 'mixed multitude' (Exodus 12:38) ..." (p.17).

Is "regenerate membership" a fact, or a fiction?

2. If there is a difference, is it merely a *quantitative* difference, i.e. a higher proportion of people with a genuine commitment to Christ in a believers' church, or is there a *qualitative* difference? In other words, does a believers' church expect a different type of spiritual experience (as a

R: Who is a Believer?

condition of membership) from that of a church with "mixed membership"?

3. If we speak of a believers' church do we not thereby suggest that the key to our concept of the church is the understanding of *faith*? Do all Christians mean the same thing by "faith"?

4. Presumably, all churches claim that their members are "believers". Then the real question is: Who is a *believer*? How does one become a believer?

To some, faith is the product of sacramental acts (Roman Catholic and Anglican concept of regeneration in the waters of baptism). To others, it is the end result of a catechetical process, i.e. intellectual indoctrination: "I subscribe to a creed." Still to others, it is a psychological response with certain emotional symptoms which can be identified as evidence of faith. To others, faith is an act of will, a surrender to a Person or Cause (Kingdom), with the overtones of moral self-improvement. On the basis of such varied interpretations of "faith", one may differentiate between several types of church membership, such as sacramental or creedal.

5. It should be recognized that all these concepts of faith have one thing in common: the emphasis on *a human act* (submission to sacramental rites, or intellectual, emotional or volitive responses). In this sense it is quite appropriate to speak of the "degrees of commitment always present in the ups and downs of a developing faith" (Groff, p. 7).

Is it not imperative to emphasize that in the Scriptures, faith—even though it represents the response of a human being to the call from God—is primarily *an act of God*? Was this not precisely the main point in the conversation between Jesus and Nicodemus concerning the new birth? "Unless one is born anew, he cannot see the kingdom of God... That which is born of the flesh is flesh, and that which is born of the Spirit is spirit." (John 3:3,6). Does not the Pauline emphasis on *sola gratia* and *sola fide* point in the same direction? "This event—Jesus on the cross—continues to intrude itself upon

Open Doors

the present with new resolves and possibilities for facing one's tomorrows. In this sense the capacity to believe is profoundly *a gift before it is a task.* It is a free act that stems from the prior grace that roots in the living event of the man on the cross". (Groff, p. 7). We would like to add to this: *and the Risen Lord.* Without the Risen Christ, there can be no Christian faith. With Paul we can say: "It is no longer I who lives, but Christ lives in me" (Gal. 2:20).

6. Faith cannot be defined merely in terms of a cognitive assent, an emotional experience, or a surrender of the will. Faith is synonymous with the reality of new birth and new nature. It represents nothing less than the *ontological* invasion of the New Age into the being of a believer and of the believing community. As such, faith is the work of the Holy Spirit.

7. If this is so, then a believers' church is humanly helpless and totally dependent upon the work of God. A denomination which is constituted on the principle of "mixed membership" and on infant baptism, can predict its numerical growth on the basis of national vital statistics. By way of contrast, a believers' church is only one generation away from extinction. Unless God the Spirit continues His gracious ministry of regeneration, such a church is doomed to death.

The courage to defend the concept of the believers' church must always be accompanied by heart-searching humility. *Corruptio optimi pessima.* Inevitably, we are exposed to the temptation of spiritual pride and self-deceit: "We have the *real* faith but others do not!" We have not been called to judge others. Nevertheless, we are being called to genuine faith.

[NOTE: The text of Warren F. Groff's paper was published in *The Concept of the Believers' Church*, ed. James Leo Garrett, Jr. (Scottdale, PA: Herald Press, 1969), pp. 60-72. A brief digest of the response by J. K. Zeman was included on pp. 59-60.]

S. THE SIGNIFICANCE OF THE CONCEPT OF THE BELIEVERS' CHURCH (1977)

Baptists belong to the free church tradition of Christianity. The free church movement had two cradles during the Reformation period: Anabaptism on the Continent, and Puritan Separatism in England. Although the two had independent origins they were similar in their concept of "the free church": (1) free from state control; (2) free from hierarchical control (congregational polity); (3) free from fixed forms of worship (rejection of liturgical uniformity) and (4) free from credal unanimity (individual freedom to interpret the Scriptures).

The free church meant also a voluntary gathering of believers in congregations (regenerate church membership rather than the parish system), the right of free exercise of religion by all persons, and the right to evangelize. The practice of separation of church and state in North America means that all denominations are "free churches" in that limited sense. For that reason, the term "believers' church" had been proposed as an alternative designation of the free church heritage. The term is open to misunderstanding in two respects. It does *not* imply the primacy of beliefs (doctrine) nor a self-righteous denial of the presence of believers in denominations which do not hold to regenerate church membership. In the positive sense, the term suggests the church as a fellowship of believers. In place of exaggerated modern religious individualism, so often confused with the free church tradition, the concept of the believers' church underscores the church as "a covenanted and disciplined community, a fellowship of mutual support and correction" (George H. Williams). Spiritual growth and maturity leads to the ministry of all believers.

In Canada and the U.S.A., both streams of the believers' church tradition are represented today. The Mennonites, the Church of the Brethren and others trace their origins to the Continent while Baptists, Quakers, Methodists and others represent the free church traditions transplanted from England. In the past, there were few contacts between the two streams.

The Believers' Church movement seeks to facilitate a meaningful dialogue between the two streams, as well as practical cooperation in such areas as relief work overseas. Furthermore, Baptist involvement in the movement can serve as a healthy and long overdue corrective to our somewhat lopsided ecumenicity which used to be limited to contacts with the United, Presbyterian and Anglican Churches. Does not the very name "ecumenical" compel us to seek fellowship with the whole Body of Christ? Are not denominations which uphold regenerate church membership our closest relatives in spite of cultural differences? To be involved in the Believers' Church Movement does not mean termination of our present ecumenical relationships but rather widening of our ecumenical horizons. The impetus for the movement was provided by several Believers' Church Conferences (Louisville, 1967; Chicago 1970; Los Angeles and Zurich, 1975) in which Canadian Baptists participated. A Study Conference on the Believers' Church in Canada is planned in Winnipeg for May, 1978.

[NOTE: A text circulated with invitations to the conference in Winnipeg.]

T. GROWING TOGETHER (1980)

Growth in Ecumenical Relations

From the beginning, Baptists have affirmed their faith in one universal church under one head, Jesus Christ. They rejected the concept of a national Protestant church, such as the Church of England or the Church of Scotland, to which every citizen automatically belonged through infant baptism. Over against it, they held up the ideal of a believers' church, "the company of the committed" (Trueblood) built in local congregations on the basis of regenerate membership symbolized by believer's baptism. Along with the concern for religious liberty, that has been and continues to be the central thrust of our distinctive witness.

In the beginning, such separate denominational existence was regarded by our fathers as only provisional, that is, necessary only until the whole church would come to respect what our fathers regarded as plain scriptural teaching. When the whole church would obey the word of God they were prepared to co-operate in the restoration of the visible unity of God's people. With such hope they were prepared to discuss issues of theology and practice with any Christian group, and to bear witness to their particular understanding of the truth. When increased religious freedom in England and America permitted it, our fathers did not hesitate to enter into co-operative projects with other Christians, such as the Bible Society.

As Canadian Baptists we have walked a path of openness and readiness for dialogue and co-operation, for most of our 220 years of history. We have not been isolationists. I have reviewed Canadian Baptist involvements in co-operative Christianity since 1900 in a booklet circulated by the Baptist Federation in 1972.[1] The information available there requires no updating except for three recent developments.

First, the Baptist Federation played a crucial role in the convocation of the first Believers' Church Conference in

Canada held in Winnipeg two years ago. The event represented a much needed broadening of the ecumenical perspectives for us and for the whole church in Canada. All papers presented at the conference have been published in the book, *The Believers' Church in Canada* (1979).[2]

Second, two of our seminaries have entered into important contracts with ecumenical significance which will affect the outlook of the new generation of pastors trained there. McMaster Divinity College co-operates closely with the Toronto School of Theology, and Carey Hall with Regent College in Vancouver. The two agreements represent different but complementary directions in ecumenical co-operation. We dare not underestimate their significance for the future Baptist identity in Canada.

Finally, the Council of the Baptist Federation of Canada found it necessary to terminate BFC membership in the Canadian Council of Churches at the end of the present calendar year. The only reason for the decision was constitutional. Since two of the four member Conventions had terminated their support of CCC (the Atlantic Convention in 1971 and the French Union in 1973), the BFC as a national body no longer had the necessary mandate to represent Baptists in the CCC. Integrity demanded the decision, delayed for several years.

Contrary to inaccurate newspaper reports, the present leaders of the Federation do not espouse isolationism. We are participating in the continuing discussions on the wider ecumenical fellowship. We shall seek to enlarge the scope of our ecumenical involvements in the 1980s. Speaking for myself, I would like to make a twofold plea for Baptist growth in ecumenical relations in the 1980s.

(1) In the New Testament, the concern for the oneness of the church is always expressed as a plea for the *whole* body of Christ, not just a segment of the body, to grow in truth and love. The term "ecumenical" conveys the same concern for the wholeness of the church. Yet in practice, for many reasons, the official ecumenical movement, institutionalized

T: Growing Together

in the regional and national Councils of Churches, such as the Canadian Council of Churches, and in the World Council of Churches, has failed up to now to involve the whole body of Christians.

Obviously, such was not and is not the intention of the leaders in the ecumenical movement. They deplore the shortcoming. In the preparatory negotiations for the wider ecumenical fellowship in Canada, invitations for participation have been sent to all Christian denominations in our country. But the fact remains that the Canadian Council of Churches does not represent the whole body of Christians in our land.

The situation is further complicated by the gradual but far-reaching changes in the composition of the Protestant family of denominations in Canada. Last year, the Canadian Church Growth Centre in Regina, headed by Dr. Dennis Oliver, now Consultant on Church Growth for the Presbyterian Church in Toronto, released the results of a national survey of participation in religious life in Canada. The survey compared figures for actual attendance of church services and Sunday Schools, rather than statistics from membership rolls.

The report suggested that it is no longer possible to speak of the so-called "main line" denominations in Canada. Why? The combined attendance in the four major pedobaptist denominations (Anglican, United, Presbyterian and Lutheran) was lower than the combined participation in the major believers' churches, such as Baptists, Mennonites and the Pentecostal Assemblies. The report sums up: On the threshold of the 1980s, "Canada is more secular, more Roman Catholic and more evangelical than is popularly recognized."[3]

The findings came as a surprise to people who are used to assess Canadian religious life by census figures of minimal attachment to churches, or by membership figures prepared by each denomination on a different basis. Should not the actual involvement in church life be used as the only reliable index of the vitality of a church? How can one be a member of the body of Christ without participation in its fellowship?

Open Doors

Whatever the reader's opinion may be of the value of these and other statistical surveys, there can be no doubt about two facts. First, in terms of reaching Canadians with the gospel of Jesus Christ, the old Protestant denominations no longer dominate the religious scene in our country as they used to. The growing edge and the greater vitality is demonstrated by the so-called smaller — no longer so small — groups upholding the principle of regenerate church membership. A radically different religious profile of Canadian population is emerging in this decade.

Second, we find ourselves, as Baptists, in the middle of the ecumenical spectrum of Canadian Protestantism, from the Anglican Church, on the one end, to Pentecostal Assemblies and Gospel Halls, on the other. Our position in the centre is at once a great opportunity, and a great risk. The risk is obvious.

We may easily become polarized into two camps: those who treasure the old ecumenical alliance with the so-called mainline Protestant churches, and those who increasingly find more meaningful fellowship in the so-called evangelical wing of Canadian Protestantism and its channels of co-operation (the Evangelical Fellowship of Canada and other organizations). If such polarization should be allowed to develop among us, it could ultimately pose a threat to our unity, both within each Convention/Union and within the Federation.

At the same time, we have a God-given mandate and opportunity to practise "wholesome" ecumenicity rather than a partial expression of it. Because of our dual roots in the beginnings of Baptist life, in the Puritan movement in England and in the Anabaptist-Mennonite fellowship on the continent; because of our long experience in coping with the dialectic tension between the church-type and sect-type of Christianity (to use Troeltsch's typology) or, if you prefer, between the centripetal and centrifugal forces in Christendom; we are, I believe, well prepared to relate to the whole body of Christ in Canada.

T: Growing Together

We have much in common with the United and Presbyterian Churches, socially, culturally, and in religious traditions. But at the same time, we share the vision of the church of born again believers with those new dynamic groups which are but beginning to make their impact upon the religious scene in Canada.

The problem we face is that most of us prefer comfortable ecumenical associations with groups and Christians with whom we are familiar, who sing the same hymns, follow similar patterns of worship, and usually belong to the same social class and cultural milieu. Is it not imperative to seek out, deliberately, the less familiar and the less comfortable ecumenical relations in the 1980s?

My plea is applicable to both directions in ecumenicity: to contacts with Roman Catholic and Eastern Orthodox Christians on the one side, and with the Mennonites, Pentecostals or the Plymouth Brethren, on the other. Enlarge your ecumenical vision! Ecumenicity involves the whole body of Christ, or it is not ecumenicity at all.

(2) My second plea is for growth in ecumenical relations at the grass roots level. The news media tend to glorify heretics and hierarchies. Heretics make headlines, and so do the bishops and the pope. But for a non-hierarchical body with congregational polity such as we are, a pronouncement by the president or the council has little significance unless it is endorsed and implemented by the local churches. But is that not where the real ecumenical growth needs to take place?

National committees and councils can issue all kinds of statements on unity but the quest for the oneness in Christ will make little progress unless it is expressed at the grass roots level. A local church can take the initiative to arrange a series of visits by, or to neighbouring congregations of other denominations, exchanges for the purpose of becoming better acquainted with one another, or engaging in joint projects of action in the community. It should be accepted as normal and

Open Doors

wholesome to relate to different denominational clusters for particular purposes.

Dare we anticipate, in bold faith, the 1980s as a watershed in Canadian Baptist ecumenical relations?

Endnotes

1. *Baptists in Canada and Cooperative Christianity* (Brantford: Baptist Federation of Canada, 1972).
2. *The Believers' Church in Canada*, ed. J. K. Zeman and W. Klaassen (n.p.: Baptist Federation of Canada and Mennonite Central Committee, 1979).
3. *The Canadian Baptist*, October 1979, p. 36.

[Note. An address presented at the assembly of the Baptist Convention of Ontario and Quebec in Hamilton, ON, June 6, 1980. The first part of the text, "Growth in Canadian Baptist Unity", is deleted here. Reprinted from *The Canadian Baptist*, October 1980, pp. 5-6.]

U. INTERFAITH INTERFACE (1984)

Opening New Doors to Fellowship with Other Christians

By its constitution, the Baptist Federation of Canada was assigned primary responsibility for national, international and interdenominational relations and "to express the common judgement of the constituent churches and organizations on such matters." Since the organization of the BFC. in 1944, most of the debates on Baptist ecumenical involvement have focused on the question of membership in the Canadian Council of Churches (CCC) and the World Council of Churches (WCC).

Without a clear directive in the BFC constitution, the right of the national Baptist body to seek membership in the CCC and the WCC was interpreted as contingent upon endorsement of such affiliation by all its constituent regional conventions/unions. Originally, such consensus made possible BFC membership in the CCC. Lack of it prevented membership in the WCC. When two of the four conventions/unions withdrew their support of affiliation with CCC, the BFC terminated its membership in 1980.

Since 1981, the BCOQ has been the Baptist member body of the CCC, an anomaly in a council of national, rather than regional, church bodies. At the present time, the BCOQ and the BUWC are exploring the question of affiliation with the Evangelical Fellowship of Canada.

In retrospect, the preoccupation with issues of affiliation in our discussions of ecumenical relations must be regretted. By and large, such a narrow focus prevented systematic attention to the real issues in the quest for Christian unity: questions of truth (differences in doctrine) and opportunities for co-operative witness and action in society.

In recent years, another trend, widespread in our circles, has further eroded our commitment to cooperation with other Christians and churches. The majority of Canadian

Baptist people appear to have been preoccupied with local church activities—which are, of course, their primary responsibility—to the neglect of their common tasks on the regional, national and international scenes. One would expect that the rising level of support for world missions (CBOMB) might lead to greater consciousness of global issues.

When the BFC found it necessary to terminate its membership in the CCC, it appointed an Inter-Church Relations Committee (ICRC), chaired by Mrs. Shirley Bentall of Calgary and later by J. K. Zeman, to give creative leadership in this important area. The ICRC has sought, first of all, to open new doors for fellowship with Christian bodies and groups *at the national level.*

From 1980 to 1982, Baptists were represented, as observers, at the conferences of Canadian Church Leaders and at meetings of the new ecumenical Inter-Church Committee (ICC). In lengthy negotiations, the Committee worked toward the formation of a new national co-operative body, with denominational participation wider than the CCC and with primary emphasis on fellowship rather than on the ecumenical agenda related to the WCC.

However, the plan to replace the CCC with an "Association of Christian Churches in Canada" was abandoned earlier this year. In March 1984, the Canadian Conference of Catholic Bishops (CCCB) made known its desire to enter into some form of associate membership in the CCC. Their decision marks the beginning of a new phase in Canadian conciliar ecumenism.

During the past four years, the ICRC of the BFC has initiated a series of informal bilateral conversations with representatives of several denominations, viz. the Council of Christian Reformed Churches in Canada, the Mennonite Central Committee, the North American Baptist Conference and the Presbyterian Church in Canada. The topics under discussion included questions of doctrine, practice and areas of possible co-operation. Among others, Dr. R. F. Aldwinckle,

U: Interfaith Interface

Dr. Paul Dekar and Dr. McCormack Smyth presented papers at the meetings.

Since Baptists stand in the middle of the Canadian denominational spectrum, the ICRC is conscious of its unique opportunity to build bridges of fellowship both with the "mainline" denominations and with the smaller evangelical bodies.

Growing in Understanding and Obedience: The Power of Truth

The search for closer fellowship with Christians from other denominational traditions inevitably exposes differences in doctrines and practices. From its beginning, the modern ecumenical movement has included on its agenda intensive theological discussions (Faith and Order Commission and Conferences).

Since World War II, Canadian Baptists have contributed several important statements to the ongoing theological conversations. The BFC published two of them: *Of Water and Spirit: A Baptist View of Church Membership* by Russell F. Aldwinckle (1964) and *A Baptist Response to the Principles of Union between the Anglican Church of Canada and the United Church of Canada* (by a committee chaired by R. F. Aldwinckle, 1970). It is worth noting that the basic Baptist distinctives, outlined in both of these statements, now reappear as the main Baptist critique of the new document issued by the WCC to its member bodies, *Baptism, Eucharist and Ministry* (BEM, 1982).

In view of the historic importance of the BEM document—being described by some theologians as a modern counterpart of the ancient ecumenical creeds—the ICRC made a request to the faculties of the four Canadian Baptist seminaries related to the CBF (Acadia, Carey Hall, CETE and McMaster) to examine and evaluate the BEM statement in the light of scriptures and the traditional Baptist interpretation. All four schools responded favourably. On 20-21 June the ICRC convened in Toronto a consultation with representatives of our seminaries. It is our hope that a Canadian Baptist statement on baptism, Lord's Supper and ministries may appear in due course as an educational tool for study in our churches across Canada.

Furthermore, several theological statements on Christian witness in the context of the modern world have been issued in recent years by the World Evangelical Fellowship (Lausanne Committee) and the Commission on World Mission and Evangelism of the WCC (*Mission and Evangelism*, 1982). At the request of the ICRC, the faculties of our seminaries are undertaking a study of these documents which spell out a theological basis for the evangelistic and missionary task of the churches around the world.

The preceding paragraphs provide a brief summary of the activities pursued by the ICRC at the national level. Like many other denominational committees, the ICRC faces the frustration of isolation from the life of local congregations. Unless there is vision of, and burden for, inter-church relations in our congregations, the work of a national committee will result in little more than a pile of papers deposited in denominational archives.

[Note. Reprinted from *The Canadian Baptist*, October 1984, pp. 14-15.]

V. REPORT AND REFLECTIONS ON THE SIXTH ASSEMBLY OF THE WORLD COUNCIL OF CHURCHES, VANCOUVER, BC,

July 24 - August 10, 1983

Outline

    Introduction

    I   Facts

        1. The Place
        2. The People
        3. The Program

    II   Impressions and Interpretation of Trends

        1. The Leaders
        2. The Main Emphases of the Assembly Program
        3. The Changing Composition and Orientation of the WCC
        4. WCC and the Roman Catholic Church
        5. WCC and Evangelicals
        6. WCC and Baptists

[Note. Only Sections 2 and 6 of Part II are reprinted here.]

2. The Main Emphases of the Assembly Program

(a) The main addresses and plenary discussions, particularly during the first half of the assembly, revolved around the twin theme of *peace and justice*. The exposure of poverty and economic exploitation, perceived as violation of human dignity and basic human rights; the condemnation of racism and militarism, especially in relation to nuclear arms; the use and abuse of political and economic power—these were the main concerns which were addressed and discussed as the top priorities on the agenda. The theme, "Jesus Christ the Life of the World", was interpreted with a predominantly "this-worldly" and social (rather than individual) application. To a large extent, addresses and discussions reflected different versions of liberation theology.

At his final press conference (August 10) Dr. Philip Potter singled out *power* and its use as the key question facing humanity today. He said he was ready to stand up and face death. "The hope for the future is the global solidarity of the oppressed and the global solidarity of churches. What a combined strength!" ...

(b) The second central thrust of the assembly was the emphasis on *sacramental unity* of the church. It was highlighted by the repeated references to the document on *Baptism, Eucharist and Ministry*, and acted out in the worship tent, particularly in the celebration of the Lima liturgy. The increased influence of the liturgical traditions (Eastern Orthodox, Roman Catholic, Anglican and Lutheran) and the diminishing role of the reformed and free church traditions in the WCC, were clearly demonstrated at the Vancouver assembly.

(c) The concern for *doctrinal consensus* (now described as "convergence" in the ecumenical vocabulary) was moved down on the list of ecumenical priorities, with the exception of BEM. The absence of "great theologians" at the assembly, and on its program, seemed to confirm that trend.

(d) The WCC constitution states that the Council "is a fellowship of churches which confess the Lord Jesus Christ as God and Saviour *according to the Scriptures* and therefore seek to fulfil together their common calling to the glory of the one God, Father, Son and Holy Spirit." There is no mention of tradition. But the reports from the Faith and Order Commission of the WCC in recent years, and statements by WCC

V. The World Council of Churches

spokespersons in Vancouver strongly suggest that the Scriptures as the norm and basis for common witness and action have been replaced with a new standard, the norm of "the holy apostolic tradition", flexible and still evolving in the process of "convergence of traditions".

This crucial shift in the theological orientation of the WCC has been signalled already at the Faith and Order Conference in Montreal in 1963, with its paradigm of normative Tradition which is expressed equally in Scriptures and the various denominational traditions. The trend provides additional evidence of the growing influence of the Eastern Orthodox and Roman Catholic churches and may suggest that the ecumenical movement has entered a post-Protestant phase.

At a press conference on August 2, William Lazareth, Director of the Faith and Order Commission of the WCC in Geneva, himself an American Lutheran, stated: "The BEM is a faithful statement of the biblical-patristic period during which the church was held together. The burden of the proof is on the churches to prove that they are related to *the holy tradition of the Gospel*." He was referring to "the process of reception" (another ecumenical in-word) of the BEM document which had been released to member churches for official response. He described the next stage in the theological discussions in the ecumenical movement as "a move from sacramental convergence to full confessional unity".

He expressed the hope that the process of reception (i.e. endorsement) of the BEM statement may lead to a global Conference on Faith and Order in 1987 to mark the 1200th anniversary of the last (seventh) ecumenical council of a united church (Nicaea II in 787). Such a conference might not yet have the weight of authority comparable to the seven ancient ecumenical councils but it may pave the way toward new confessional unity in Christendom.

In a comment on the position of the Reformed churches within WCC, Dr. Lazareth said, "they must decide what constitutes the core of the Reformed tradition." It is crucial to note that in all of his comments there was no reference to the authority of *Scriptures*, given to the church and acknowledged by it (both in the early patristic and in the Reformation periods) as the unchanging record of God's revealed truth and the norm of doctrine and practice by which the evolving traditions of churches must be judged and continually reformed.

The place of Scriptures at the Vancouver assembly would merit a more thorough investigation and assessment. Suffice it to say that it was ambivalent. On the one hand, the Bible as a book was given a place of prominence in the ceremonial procession of the opening worship on July 24, and most liturgical celebrations in the worship tent were saturated with Scripture readings (not always accompanied by exposition). The address by the General Secretary was a powerful demonstration of exegetical preaching rather than a typical administrative report.

On the other hand, the program, as a whole, lacked daily exposition, and consistent application of biblical teaching to the various concerns of the WCC. References to the diverse ecclesial traditions, and appeals to the one common and normative apostolic tradition (whatever that may mean to the various branches of Christendom) could be heard more frequently than appeals to the scriptural norm.

For Baptists and for other Protestants in the free church tradition, as the people of one Book, with no binding confessions, no prescribed liturgies, no uniform church order, but with personal freedom of interpretation and with congregational autonomy in all aspects of church life, the trends perceived at the WCC assembly raise many questions about the changing directions of the ecumenical movement.

(e) The individual appropriation of the assembly theme (Jesus Christ, the Life of the World) in the sense of *personal salvation*, with the ensuing assurance of *eternal* life, was almost totally ignored, even in most "personal testimonies" included on the program. There were three notable exceptions: the address of Bishop Festo Kivengere from Uganda and the

V. The World Council of Churches

short testimonies by David du Plessis (U.S.A.) and Peter Kuzmic (Jugoslavia), both Pentecostal Christians.

The emphasis on collective and "this worldly" meaning of salvation may be a healthy corrective to the individualism of traditional Protestant piety. But if it is carried to the opposite extreme, it becomes an equally dangerous distortion of the biblical teaching, with its balance of personal experience of regeneration, and incorporation into the body of Christ, the church.

(f) The call to personal witnessing as the central task of the church in evangelism and mission (Acts 1:8) was not the topic of any *major* address or other form of presentation, with one exception (the encounter between the two positions on "The Gospel and Salvation" at Public Forum No. 1, between bishop Festo Kivengere from Uganda and Dr. Alan Boesak of South Africa, on July 27). Whereas the BEM document received repeated recognition, the other major statement released in 1982 by the Central Committee of the WCC to its member churches for response, *Mission and Evangelism: An Ecumenical Affirmation*, was hardly mentioned at all, perhaps as an embarrassment in the presence of official guests from other world religions and the promoted dialogue with them. Besides, Eastern Orthodox churches have often regarded Protestant evangelism as proselytism.

(g) The concern for *freedom* from economic oppression (exploitation) was not matched by equal burden for freedom from political oppression and from *religious persecution* by whatever regime. One can understand the political sensitivity in this area of concern. Yet in spite of many voices pleading at the assembly for equal condemnation of violation of basic human rights wherever it occurs, such impartial stance could not be fully achieved in Vancouver.

(h) Several pressing but *divisive issues* on which consensus cannot be achieved among the WCC member bodies at the present time, were deliberately avoided on the assembly agenda and in the discussions. The General Secretary publicly admitted such policy. The list of such topics include abortion, celibacy of priests, divorce, euthanasia, homosexuality and ordination of women. With the dominant application of the assembly theme to issues of life and death in contemporary society, one would expect the assembly to take an unequivocal stand on abortion and euthanasia, as the Roman Catholic Church has done.

6. The WCC and Baptists

Eleven Baptist conventions/unions, all affiliated with the BWA and member bodies of the WCC, were represented at the Vancouver assembly by delegates, as follows:

Africa	Nigerian Baptist Convention	3 delegates
Asia	Burma Baptist Convention	3
Oceania	Baptist Union of New Zealand	1
Europe	B. Union of Great Britain & Ireland	3
	Union of Evang. Christian-Baptists U.S.S.R.	3
	Baptist Union of Denmark	1
	Baptist Union of Hungary	1
N. America	American Baptist Churches	5
	Three Black Baptist Conventions* (National B. Conv. of America, National B. Conv., U.S.A., Inc., Progressive Ntl. B. Conv., Inc.)	13

— — — — — — — — — —

A total of 33 delegates out of 838 present.

— — — — — — — — — —

*   The official list of delegates did not differentiate between the three conventions.

Another Baptist Convention, from Nicaragua, was admitted to membership in Vancouver. The group of the twelve Baptist conventions in nine countries represents a small number out of the total 124 member bodies of the Baptist World

V. The World Council of Churches

Alliance in 92 nations and dependencies (1983). But the combined membership of the twelve constitutes more than a third of the BWA membership, and certainly an influential minority within the BWA. There are, of course, many other Baptist bodies which are not affiliated with the BWA.

[Note. Reprinted from the paper, "Sixth Assembly of the World Council of Churches, Vancouver, B.C., July 24-August 10, 1983" (mimeographed), pp. 7-10 and 14.]

PART SEVEN:
CONCEPT OF MINISTRY AND MINISTERIAL TRAINING

W. HOW TO TRAIN GOOD MINISTERS (1957)

It was my privilege to take part as guest in the second *Conference of European Baptist Theological Teachers* which was held on the lovely campus of the International Baptist Seminary in Ruschlikon, Switzerland, on March 20-23, 1957. Thirty-five professors and teachers were in attendance, with a few Baptist leaders added from countries where at present there is no Baptist training centre.

[Information on particular countries is deleted here.]

It is not my intention to give a detailed summary of the several excellent addresses, nor of the reports on Baptist theological training in different countries, nor of the discussions. Any one interested may obtain such information from the official minutes of the BWA's sub-committee. Rather, I would attempt to underline some of the problems which the Baptist, and indeed all Christian churches in the whole western world, face in ministerial training.

The Goals in Theological Education

Principal R. C. Child (Regent's Park College, Oxford) offered the following threefold definition: (a) to develop and train the individual mind of the students, (b) to place at their disposal the chief skills for their future service, (c) to fortify and elevate their character as Christian men. In other words, the development of a mature Christian person within the community of fellow students, teachers and church members is far more important than the mere imparting of factual knowledge. The purpose of theological education is "to kindle a fire, not to fill a pot"; hence the British stress on strictly residential theological colleges with a minimum of lectures and a maximum of personal tuition, and of individual assignments of study. The continental Baptists found themselves in agreement with this definition, with the added emphasis, perhaps, on the development of the evangelistic abilities of the students.

The Best Methods

1. Modern society, just as much in Britain and Europe as in America, is falling a victim to an ever increasing *specialization* of life. How far should this trend be reflected in the training of ministers? How to strike a happy medium between a solid core of basic theological training, particularly in the biblical fields, and the specialized courses for missionaries, chaplains in hospitals, armed forces, industry etc., youth leaders, for educational work, journalism or radio work? Does the "basic core" include a working knowledge of Hebrew and Greek? The British tradition has laid a great stress on a thorough knowledge of the biblical languages as the basic tool with which the minister has to work, while the Continental and American Baptist concept of theological education seems to subordinate it to the training in the practical skills of the ministry.

2. The question of method extends, of course, beyond the problems of the curriculum. What proportion of time should the student in training spend in the classroom and in his study, and how much time should he devote to *field work*? In Germany no student can be enrolled in the seminary without a minimum of one year's full time experience as leader in one of the many Baptist social institutions, such as youth homes, or hostels. Some American seminaries have adopted an "internship" year during which the student is engaged in full time work under the supervision of his teachers; it can either be inserted between the second and the last year of the theological course, or follow immediately after the graduation. Preaching on weekends, or serving as student pastors, is a generally accepted practice both in Britain and on the Continent although in most cases it would not be required.

3. *The devotional life* in the seminary and the whole atmosphere of the school may well be seen as of more lasting influence on the student's future ministry than the impress of

W. How to Train Ministers

the factual theological knowledge itself. "It is the atmosphere that makes the earth habitable. It is the atmosphere that makes the theological college profitable." In England, the faculty and students join in a monthly, or even weekly communion. The importance of the nearby churches in which the students worship, was underlined by Dr. H. Luckey (Hamburg, Germany): "the spiritually strongest ministers of the whole denomination should be near the seminary so that the students may find regularly an inspiring ideal for their own ministry as well as true refreshment and renewal of their devotion to the Lord."

4. The problem of *recruiting* a sufficient number of candidates obviously does not plague all Baptists. From Denmark Dr. J. Norgaard reported an adequate supply of new students. In Germany and Spain about twice the number of young men are seeking to enter into the Baptist ministry than could be trained and placed in service. The Southern Baptist surplus of ministers is well-known. In other countries, however, an increase in the number of candidates is desirable. The Swedish Baptists require about one student in training per 1,000 members of their constituency.

5. The long debate on *standards*, curriculum, and requirements for entrance and graduation, only revealed the great variety of Baptist training institutions in Europe. Whereas the Baptist colleges in Britain are linked closely with the local universities and offer degree courses exclusively through them, on the Continent the only school with a standard B.D. course is the Ruschlikon Seminary, supported by the Southern Baptists and patterned after their schools. The other Baptist institutions in Europe have been unable so far to set uniform entrance requirements and to provide adequate faculties. One must hasten to stress, however, that in most cases such academic "defects" have by no means meant the production of an inferior ministry. It was emphasized again and again that a man trained at a Bible College type of school may well be better fitted for effective ministry among the masses than one adorned with first-class university degrees. The clergy of many European state churches might

serve as a warning. There is, nevertheless, a common trend among the Continental Baptists gradually to raise the educational standards of their ministry.

6. A plan for the formation of *an association of European Baptist theological schools* was rejected as premature under the present circumstances. Many practical suggestions, such as interchange of students and teachers, a system of mutual accrediting, and more regular sharing of information, were presented and favourably received. In particular, *the great need for developing Baptist (systematic) theology* was stated both by the Continental and the British brethren. When confronted with the well thought-out presentations of Lutheran, Reformed and other theologies, the Baptist student is groping in uncertainty, and is even unable to refer to some up-to-date Baptist printed work on the subject. All in all, the Conference was a most profitable experience for all participants, and meant a great step forward in the growing sense of unity among the European Baptists. It was agreed to hold the next conference again at Ruschlikon in two years' time.

The Concept of Ministry

The more reports we heard and the greater opportunity we had for exchange of information and opinion, the more obvious it became that ultimately all problems of theological education are related to the basic question of *our concept of ministry*. The three evening addresses, "The Ministry in Biblical Perspective" by *Dr. H. Luckey*, Germany, "The Ministry in Historical Perspective" by *Dr. E. A. Payne*, England, and "The Ministry in Contemporary Perspective" by *Dr. J. Norgaard*, Denmark, helped to focus our attention on this central issue.

The studies pursued at our seminaries and colleges can never be regarded as an end in themselves but rather as a means towards the one goal: to provide the best possible training of men and women *in view of the tasks and demands* which they will have to fulfil in their respective spheres of service. Thus a solution to these manifold problems can only be sought in a continuous conversation between the theological teachers and the rank and file members of our churches:

W. How to Train Ministers

Whom do you consider to be a "good" — not necessarily a "successful" in the "American" sense of the word — minister? Which aspect of the ministry do you expect and appreciate most: effective preaching, efficient pastoral care, educational abilities as Bible teacher, a sociable nature, work in the community's public life, and which others beside?

The answers will, of course, vary with the size and location of the church. The marks of a good rural minister will be somewhat different from those of a man serving in an industrial city area, a mining district or a church near the university campus. The faculty of a good Baptist theological school will have sensitive ears to listen to the varying and changing demands of our churches and to adjust the scheme of training promptly in accordance with them.

In the perspective of church history this represents a marked development from the one-sided emphasis of the Reformation period on the "Ministry of the Word and Sacraments", as well as from the dangerous Continental concept of "academic theology" of the last century, towards the original riches of the apostolic ministry portrayed in the New Testament. After all, the Christian ministry is not the service of the "clergy" but *the ministry of the Church as a whole*. "And his gifts to the Church were that some should be apostles, some prophets, some evangelists, some pastors and teachers, for the equipment of the saints, for the work of ministry, for building up the body of Christ, until we all attain to the unity of the faith and of the knowledge of the fullness of Christ" (Eph. 4:11-13).

Thus, one need not be surprised at the striking affinity of the *two definitions* of the task of the Christian ministry discussed at the conference. Dr. E. A. Payne quoted a statement from the High Anglican tradition: the supreme goal of a minister is "to foster in the 'laity' the deepest possible understanding of *their priesthood as 'laity'*". Dr. Jesse J. Northcutt (Fort Worth, Texas), on the other hand, referred to the recent American survey of ministerial training. The findings were summed up by its director, Dr. H. Richard Niebuhr, in the slogan: the primary function of an American minister today is that of a *"pastoral director"*, i.e. one who by his leadership and service coordinates the varied forms and spheres of Christian service rendered by his congregation as a whole. Despite their contrast in ecclesiastical and contextual origin, these two definitions point to the same revised concept of ministry.

Does it express our Canadian Baptist needs? Perhaps the fragmentary report may serve as a starter for a profitable interchange of ideas between the members of our churches, our older and younger ministers, and last but not least, the faculties and committees responsible for Canadian Baptist ministerial training. The conference did not overlook the multiple tasks of a theological college, viz. to serve as a centre of theological learning in general, to equip laymen and women for Christian service, besides training candidates for the ordained ministry, but it limited itself almost exclusively to the last mentioned.

[NOTE: Reprinted from *The Canadian Baptist*, May 15, 1957, pp. 7 and 11. The report on the conference is included in this volume to show how many of the current concepts in North American theological education were advocated in Britain and Europe more than thirty years ago.]

X. PARTNERSHIP IN MINISTRIES (1987)

The Protestant Reformation of the 16th century revised but did not reject the medieval concept of the parish priest. The "magisterial" Reformers (Lutheran, Reformed and Anglican) by and large preserved the Constantinian heritage of a "Christian society" in which citizenship and church membership overlapped. The confessional fragmentation of Europe did not upset, with a few exceptions, the principle of territorial religious uniformity at the local level. Some areas or cities became Lutheran, or Reformed, others remained Catholic. The role of the Lutheran or Reformed parish minister was patterned after the model of the medieval Roman Catholic priest except for the shift in emphasis from sacramental (liturgical) functions to the tasks of preaching and pastoral care.

1. The Traditional Task of the Protestant Minister.

The free church groups (the Continental Anabaptists and the English Congregationalists and Baptists) rejected the parish idea and sought to recover the New Testament concept of the church as a gathered community of committed disciples ("the believers' church"). Nonetheless, in their understanding of the ministry, they did not depart significantly from the pattern set by Luther and Calvin. Most Baptist confessions defined two ministerial offices. The bishops or elders (i.e. pastors) were "to dispense the word and the sacraments" while the deacons were appointed "to attend to the affairs of the poor and sick brethren" (John Smyth, 1609).

In their call for the priesthood of all believers the Reformers rejected the mediatorial role of the priest as a father confessor (penance) and agent of other sacramental graces. Among Baptists, it resulted in the central emphasis on soul liberty: direct access to God by every Christian. However, the concept of the priesthood of believers was not implemented on the horizontal level and therefore did not affect the structures and functions of Protestant ministry.

2. The Many Roles of the Contemporary Pastor.

The changing society in North America produced new types of ministry, such as itinerant evangelists, circuit riders, and more recently, chaplains, denominational secretaries and area ministers. However, the role of the local pastor remained basically unchanged until the end of the Second World War. Since then, in a climate of rapid changes, innumerable new roles have been added without any reduction or modification of the traditional functions of the preacher and pastor.

The typical urban pastor is expected to excel as "the organization man/woman" who initiates and co-ordinates the countless new groups and organizations in the local church. His/her performance is sometimes evaluated by the results of his/her efforts in fund raising and church (edifice) building. As "the publicity person" and "mass media person" he/she must produce a steady stream of church bulletins and newsletters, and project an attractive image of the church as a radio and TV personality.

As "the community leader" he/she is under pressure to become involved in several community clubs and organizations, attend their meetings and promote their objectives. As "the denominational person" he/she cannot escape the cobweb of committees and sub-committees at associational, convention and national levels. As "the ecumenical leader" he/she is expected to fraternize with ministers of other denominations for dialogue and action. The latest role that is being impressed upon ministers is that of "an agent of social change" who initiates, by word and deed, campaigns against social injustices in areas such as poverty, housing, or human rights.

On the sideline, some ministers manage to serve as unpaid counsellors, welfare agents and part-time chaplains in jails and hospitals. In addition to all these chosen and as-

X: Partnership in Ministries

signed roles, most Protestant ministers still have the courage to become spouses and parents.

The end result of such an incredible accumulation of new roles — with limited or no training for them — is only too obvious. What else can one expect but a confused self-image, fatigue and frustration, loneliness and marital tensions, disillusionment and escape into other vocations?

3. The Biblical Concept of Ministries.

For such practical reasons, and in obedience to the scriptural norm, the old image of the Protestant minister must be discarded and replaced by the New Testament concept of multiple ministries which are carried out by all members of the congregation.

A careful study of the New Testament will show that the central task of the church is *witness and service to Jesus Christ* (Mt. 4:19; Mt. 28:19-20; John 20:21; Acts 1:8; II Cor. 5:17-21 and other passages). The life of the early Christian community, as described in the Acts of the Apostles, was characterized by the following marks of the church: *didache (training for witness), koinonia* (communion, fellowship, *witness by being* a new community in Christ; life of sharing), *kerygma* (proclamation, *witness in words*), *diakonia* (service, *witness in deeds*) and *dynamis* (the power of *the Spirit*).

The New Testament epistles contain several lists of the so-called *charismatic gifts* which are bestowed by God upon *every* true member of the body of Christ in order to equip him/her for some particular ministry (service). Cf. Rom. 12:4-8; I Cor. 7:7 and 12:1-11, 27-31; I Cor. 14:26-33; Eph. 4:11-13; I Tim. 4:14; II Tim. 1:6; I Peter 4:10-11. No doubt, God provides additional gifts, not mentioned in the New Testament, for the ministries of the church to meet the changing situations and needs. However, an examination of these lists will suggest that the equipping gifts may be arranged in categories which correspond to the marks of the church. One can thus speak of a *didactic, koinonic, kerygmatic and diakonic ministries of the church.* They belong to the whole church and must be carried out by *all members* of the church.

4. Partnership in Ministries: Pastor and People.

It is generally recognized that the New Testament writings record a variety of concepts and practices in the ministries as they developed, under the guidance of the Spirit, in different geographical areas and under varying circumstances in the early church. The traditional *three* orders of professional (ordained) ministry which began to emerge in the post-apostolic age and are continued in several Christian communions today (*bishop, presbyter and deacon*) are presumably based on the New Testament. Cf. Acts 11:30; 14:23; 15:2, 4, 22-23; 16:4; 19:22; 20:17, 28; 21:18; Phil. 1:1; I Tim. 3:1-13; 4:14; 5:17; Titus 1:5-9; I Peter 5:1.

Baptists and other Protestants have insisted that the terms "bishop" (overseer, supervisor) and "elder" were often used, in the New Testament times, interchangeably (cf. Acts 20:17 and 28). It is important to note that these categories are *never included in the lists of charismatic gifts*. One might, therefore, suggest that the three categories describe *"functional (official, professional) ministries"* in contra-distinction to the "professing charismatic ministries." To put it in other words: "Ministry in the New Testament Church is completely comprehended by two functions: service and supervision" (John K. S. Reid).

The "professional" minister has the task of supervision and co-ordination of the multiple ministries which are carried out by all members of the church. Needless to say, no "professional" minister should be *merely* a co-ordinator. As a member of the body of Christ, he/she too has been equipped with particular gifts from God. Furthermore, he/she has received professional training, especially for the preaching, teaching and prophetic ministry of the word of God, and for the pastoral ministry of prayer and counselling.

A clear understanding of this dual pattern of ministry in the New Testament should enable us, in our generation, to

X: Partnership in Ministries

move, *gradually*, to a new concept and practice of professional ministry. The "new" pastor is not a "jack-of-all-trades," untrained for many of his/her added duties, and suffering from a complex of inferiority in the company of well-trained specialists among his/her lay people. Instead, he/she is the coordinator, enabler, "coach of the team," a true servant-leader.

The concept raises important questions about *the leadership style of the pastor*, or of the ministerial team. Is he/she called by the congregation to accept and implement its decisions, coordinate its activities and *conform* to its traditions? Or, is he/she also called of God to be *a reformer and transformer*, to challenge the congregational traditions? How does the pastor strike a balance between a sense of identification with his or her people, and a sense of detachment from his/her congregation, in order to act as a servant of *the Lord* rather than a mere minister of *the church*? To what extent is the style of leadership determined by his/her personality?

Any pastor who complains about the lack of response by the congregation to his/her pleas for changes after only one or two years of ministry, should be reminded that from the perspective of any congregation, *ministers come and go* — some in greater hurry than others—whereas *the church remains*. An unwise pastor can create confusion and disunity in the church, and then simply leave. Who picks up the pieces? This, too, is an important dimension of leadership.

5. The Potential for Better Ministries.

In practical terms, this means that the *first* task of the pastor (working in consultation with the deacons or a special committee) is *to discern the gifts* in the members of the congregation, and to develop, through observation and interviews, an ongoing *inventory* of the gifts for the total ministry of the church. Such an inventory (available on file for successive pastors) will make it possible to enlist the right persons for the specific tasks. A thorough biblical exposition of the concept should precede any attempts of implementation.

Open Doors

The *second* major task of the pastor is to lead the congregation in a process of streamlining the organizational structures of the local church so that the largest number of "lay ministers" will be released from the "maintenance jobs" on church machinery (organization) for the "productive" tasks of witness and service in the community. Specific projects may be accomplished by short-term task forces rather than by continuing committees.

The *third* and most important task of the professional minister is to arrange for *enabling training* of all members according to their gifts. To suggest that one person can develop the manifold gifts present among his people would mean nothing less than to revert to the old image of "jack-of-all-trades". An adequate training of the "laity" (the people of God) for their service will require *team ministries* among professional ministers, closer co-operation between neighbouring churches, additional roles for the seminaries, and development of other leadership resources.

We thus envisage an exciting new role for the *"general practitioner"* among professional ministers. He/she will work closely in *team ministries* with other professional ministers and in *shared ministries* with his/her people. There will be an increasing demand for *"specialist ministers"*, particularly in the large metropolitan areas. The churches will need specialists in *kerygmatic* ministries (mass media communicators, evangelists, drama writers and directors, and others), in *didactic* ministries (specialized training), in *koinonic* ministries (directors of small group movements, retreats, camps, etc.) and in *diakonic* ministries (chaplains in correctional and health institutions, social workers, day care centres, etc.). There is an urgent need for *short-term task forces* which will make available to churches leadership teams for various evangelistic and diakonic projects, such as coffee houses, drop-in centres, summer or winter resort ministries, and many others.

The increasing numbers of men and women, younger and older, who are answering God's call to full-time ministry, need not be perceived as a potential surplus of ministers but

X: Partnership in Ministries

rather as the raised finger of God by which he reminds his people: Can you see the many fields, in Canada and abroad, which are ripe for harvesting? Can you feel the crying needs of people around you and in distant places? Here are men and women ready to go. Confirm their calling and send them out!

[Note. Reprinted from *The Canadian Baptist*, September 1987, pp. 4-6.]

Open Doors

Y. A PLEA FOR WHOLENESS IN THEOLOGICAL EDUCATION (1990)

As I approach my retirement, I find myself reflecting frequently on my experiences at Acadia Divinity College and Acadia University. During the twenty-three years, God showered many blessings on me and my family. My wife and three of our four children graduated from Acadia University. Many new doors for research, teaching, preaching, and leadership among Canadian Baptists and far beyond, were opened to me through the encouragement and support of the four Principals under whom I was privileged to serve: Dr. Millard R. Cherry (1968-71), Dr. Abner J. Langley (1971-75), Dr. Harold L. Mitton (1975-85) and Dr. Andrew D. MacRae (since 1985).

Words are inadequate to describe the benefits derived from the happy relationships with faculty members, students and office staff persons. The amazing growth of the school, in every aspect of its development, has made it one of the very attractive places in Canada for ministerial training today. It is not my intention to review the progress made in the past. Rather, I would like to express *three major concerns* about theological education and ministerial training in the 1990s. My comments apply not only to our school but also to other Protestant institutions of theological education in North America.

I Ministerial Training in Biblical Times

There were no seminaries in biblical times. Nevertheless, one can find models in the Scriptures from which to derive general goals and guidelines for a wholesome training of ministers and missionaries. In the Old Testament era, the prophets, such as Elijah, and the circles of their disciples, can be perceived as early prototypes of preparation for ministry.

The best model in the New Testament is the "seminary" which Jesus developed for the inner circle of his followers. He

Y. A Plea for Wholeness

did not have to raise budgets, maintain buildings, nor attend board and committee meetings. The Gospels record how Jesus called particular persons, (1) "to be with him", in order to observe and learn from his example of prayer life, and from his teaching, preaching, healing and other ministries; (2) "to be sent out" to undertake similar ministries; and then (3) to report their experiences for evaluation (Matthew 10, and Luke 10). The "seminary" of Jesus was "peripatetic": he and his students walked around the country, always in touch with persons with spiritual and physical needs. Such "supervised field education" provided the basis for instruction.

The Day of Pentecost (Acts 2) marked the "graduation" from Jesus' seminary. The disciples did not receive diplomas, nor degrees. Jesus equipped them with something far more essential to a fruitful ministry. His promise, "You will receive power when the Holy Spirit comes upon you, and you will be my witnesses..." (Acts 1:8) was fulfilled that day. The wavering and timid disciples were transformed into bold apostles (missioners) with clear convictions and costly compassion.

There is nothing original in the North American "new model" for theological education which seeks to achieve a balance between the three ingredients of ministerial training: (1) knowledge of Scriptures, church history and theology, as a basis for mature discernment and leadership; (2) training in the methods and skills of ministerial work; and (3) spiritual growth (formation). The contemporary "search for wholeness" in theological education represents a long overdue return to the pattern of training provided by Jesus.

II Three Concerns for Today and Tomorrow

1. Balance Between the "Theoretical" and "Practical" Training in the Curriculum

The opportunities for church growth, and for an increasing number of specialized ministries in the context of the North American society, exert a pressure on seminaries to provide more diversified training in the practical skills for ministry. These demands have led to a substantial increase in the offerings of "practical" courses, and to a corresponding growth of faculty in such fields.

During the 1990-91 academic year, students at Acadia Divinity College could choose from *eight elective courses* in the "theoretical" disciplines (Old and New Testaments, Church History, and Theology). At the same time, the menu of *electives* in the "practical" subjects listed *twenty-four courses*. When I began my teaching ministry at Acadia in 1968, there were four full-time faculty members in the four "academic" disciplines (listed above), and only two full-time professors in the "practical" fields. At the present time (1990-91) there are still only four full-time faculty members in the "theoretical" fields, whereas the number of professors in the "practical" subject areas has increased from two to eight, and there will likely be more appointments. Similar trends are reported from other schools.

Admittedly, one can exaggerate the dichotomy between the "theoretical" and the "practical" disciplines in ministerial training. The two categories are being integrated increasingly through such provisions as interdisciplinary courses. Nonetheless, *the balance* in the course offerings and faculty composition in many North American seminaries has been dangerously disturbed. The implications of the shift in curricular emphasis for the next generation of ministers cannot be overestimated.

The churches and seminaries must respond to the changing needs of the people. However, should not more of the increasing specialization in the training of ministers be implemented through programs of continuing education, or further graduate studies, rather than in the foundational seminary curriculum (M.Div. and M.R.E. programs)? A recent statement by the former General Secretary of the Canadian Bible Society, Dr. Kenneth G. McMillan—who can hardly be labelled as "an academic theologian"—underscores the need for greater balance in contemporary theological curriculum so that the seminary graduates are better equipped to cope with the theological illiteracy and spiritual impotence among church members.

Y. A Plea for Wholeness

False theology lies at the root of the decline in the Canadian Churches. Theology does not have a high priority today. The evangelical churches are no exception. Much Bible study has a weak theological base. In worship without theology, sound doctrine degenerates into entertainment. Genuine Christian action is based on theological convictions about the nature of God, of humanity and of this world. Without sound theology the Christian faith becomes both fruitless and rootless.[1]

2. Balance Between Inner-Directed and Outer-Directed Ministries in Ministerial Training

The concept of ministry which Jesus exemplified and for which he trained his disciples was not modelled after the priestly service in temple worship, with its predictable routine of rituals, and in a safe, fortress-like setting. Rather, he dispatched them on a mission in society, as messengers with the Good News, and as helpers with divine empowerment to heal both souls and bodies. They were sent out to contact, confront, or comfort persons with an endless variety of needs and, more often than not, in unpredictable situations. That is why Jesus promised: "I am with you always—wherever you go."

Too many contemporary congregations are preoccupied with activities inside their comfortable church buildings (the inner-directed ministries). Therefore, they have little, if any, human and other resources left for the outer-directed ministries: outreach to the community, country, and through global missions, to the whole world. It appears that the present curriculum in many seminaries reinforces and perpetuates the concentration on the inner-directed ministries.

Without evangelism as the top priority in the ministries of both the pastor and his/her people, the future is bleak for any Baptist church. Unless new persons are brought face to face with Jesus Christ, and helped to surrender their lives to him, there can be no genuine church growth for a Baptist church—if it accepts and practises regenerate membership. Transfers of membership can camouflage, for a while, the lack of primary church growth. But without evangelism, many small Baptist churches will disappear.

3. Balance Between the Vertical and Horizontal Dimensions

Dr. James Houston of Regent College, Vancouver, is reported to have said: "It is easier to get a Ph.D. than to become a person of prayer." Martin Luther condemned the dependence of the late medieval church upon sacraments as the exclusive channels for the flow of God's grace. He described it as "the Babylonian captivity of the church". Could it be that in our day, churches and ministers, seminaries and professors, are *trapped in an horizontal captivity* when they fail to live in the presence of, and by empowerment from God?

The strong trend to *professionalism* in theological education in recent years often leads to a weakening of the vertical dimension. Professionals, in various fields of human endeavour, usually operate with a high degree of self-confidence in their spheres of competence. Busy pastors who serve primarily as counsellors, social workers, promoters and administrators of programs, have little time left for disciplined study of the Bible and for a life of prayer. They really do not need God to disrupt their planned pursuits and schedules.

The fallacy of such "horizontal captivity" is obvious. In most larger communities, there are specialists with superior training in their particular fields. The unique expertise of a Christian minister surely lies elsewhere. He/she is usually the only person in the community who is trained in competent exposition of the Scriptures, with the knowledge of the original languages; a person with theological discernment in the field of religious experience; and, above all, a person who is in touch with God through a life of prayer, and empowered by Him to serve as His messenger and ambassador.

One cannot control the Holy Spirit, and his ministry, by human means and methods. I have an uneasy feeling about the

Y. A Plea for Wholeness

term "spiritual formation" which many Protestant seminaries are borrowing from the Roman Catholic tradition of spirituality. On the basis of my study, and personal contacts with representatives of that tradition, I question the effectiveness of that model for the training of ministers and priests. There are other models of life in God, with devotional depth, both in the Bible and in the history of the church, which are more compatible with the free church tradition.

An experience early in my pastoral ministry left an indelible impression on me and my concept of ministry. A well-dressed lady came to see me one day, and shared her pilgrimage, as well as her current problems. I was very young, with limited pastoral experience. I felt incompetent to disentangle her web of confusion, and possible illness. I suggested to her to seek the advice of a medical doctor, or a psychologist. She looked at me, with a mixture of disappointment and rebuke, and then, after a long pause of silence, she asked: "Well, aren't you a man of God?"

Through the long years of my varied ministries, her question has lingered in my memory and conscience. Am I a man of God, or just a practitioner of religion and theology?

Endnote

1. "Fruitless, Toothless, and Rootless," *The Presbyterian Record*, September 1990, p. 6.

[Note. The text of this address is an edited version of selected parts from two related messages which were delivered, from notes, on the following occasions: (1) the annual meeting of the Acadia Divinity College Alumni Association in Wolfville on October 15, 1990; and (2) a service in the chapel of Acadia Divinity College on November 14, 1990.]

APPENDICES

APPENDIX I
LIST OF ABBREVIATIONS

ADC	Acadia Divinity College
BCOQ	Baptist Convention of Ontario and Quebec
BJA	Baptist Jubilee Advance (program emphasis, 1959-1964)
BFC	Baptist Federation of Canada (changed to CBF in 1983)
BUWC	Baptist Union of Western Canada
BWA	Baptist World Alliance
BWMS	Baptist Women's Missionary Society of Ontario and Quebec
CB	*Canadian Baptist* (periodical, BCOQ and BUWC)
CBC	Canadian Broadcasting Corporation
CBF	Canadian Baptist Federation (changed from BFC in 1983)
L & V	*Link and Visitor* (periodical, BWMS)
UBCAP	United Baptist Convention of the Atlantic Provinces (changed from "Maritime Provinces" in 1963)
UBWMU	United Baptist Women's Missionary Union of the Atlantic Provinces

APPENDIX II

BIOGRAPHICAL TABLE

Note. The table includes only conferences and other events where I took part in the program, unless noted otherwise. References to numbers in *Bibliography* designate entries in Appendix III and IV. The omission of such references means that the material was not published. References to Selections A to Y refer to materials in this volume (*Open Doors*).

I. THE ROOTS IN EUROPE, 1926-48

A. The Personal Pilgrimage		B. The Political Context	
1926	February 27: born at Semonice, a village in Bohemia, Czechoslovakia	1918-38	Czechoslovak Republic (Western Democracy)
1932-37	Elementary School	1933	Adolf Hitler gains power in Germany
1937-45	Realne gymnasium in Jaromer (High School & Jr. College)	1938	September: Annexation of Sudetenland by Germany (Treaty of Munich)
1939	June: confirmation and full membership in the Presbyterian (Reformed) Church	1939	March 15: occupation by German Forces ("Protectorate")
		1939	September: World War II begins
1941	May: Conversion. Cf. Bibliography, No. 1, and Selection A.		

1944-45	September to April: forced labour in war industry		
1945	July-September: completion of Gymnasium (matriculation diploma)	1945	May: Liberation by Soviet and American forces; Czechoslovakia reestablished, as a Socialist Democratic Republic
1945-46	October to June: student at Charles' University in Prague (Arts)		
1946-48	Student at the Hus Theological Faculty and the University		
1948	June 15: *Cand. theol.* diploma	1948	February: Communists gain control of Czechoslovakia
	July: receives scholarship for theological studies at Knox College, Toronto		

II. TRANSPLANTATION TO CANADA, 1948, AND PASTORAL MINISTRY, 1949-59

1948-49   September to April: full-time studies (B.D.) at Knox College, Toronto

1949   April 12: Certificate of Graduation in Theology (Knox College)

April: decision to stay in Canada

May 29: baptized (by immersion), and member of the Czechoslovak Baptist Church in Toronto.

Appendix II: Biographical Table

A. MAY 1949-JANUARY 1955: ASSISTANT PASTOR, THEN PASTOR OF THE CZECHOSLOVAK BAPTIST CHURCH, TORONTO

1950 May 30: Examination and Ordination for Ministry, Toronto Association of Baptist Churches (BCOQ): Cf. Bibliography, No. 1, and Selection A.

July 18-21: Czechoslovak Baptist Convention (U.S.A. and Canada) annual assembly in Cleveland, OH.

July 22-27: 8th BWA Congress in Cleveland, OH.

1951 June 18: marriage to Lillian (nee Koncicky) in Esterhazy, SK.

June 26-July 16: tour of Baptist churches in Haiti to assess opportunities for mission work. Cf. Bibliography, No. 52.

1952 April 29: B.D. degree awarded by Knox College (after additional part-time studies, 1949-52).

September 7: Relocation of the Czechoslovak Baptist congregation from Beverley St. church building to the renovated Bethlehem Baptist Church, Rhodes Ave., Toronto. Cf. Bibliography, Nos. 3, 5 and 55, and Selection B.

October-November: Tour of Czechoslovak Baptist churches in the U.S.A. (report on mission to Haiti).

1952-81 Contributor of Czech sermon scripts for International Service (radio), Canadian Broadcasting Corporation.

1953 September 4-7: 8th Congress of the National Union of Czechoslovak Protestants in the U.S.A. and Canada, in Chicago, IL. Reelected regional vice-president for Eastern Canada.

1954 July 2-8: Czechoslovak Baptist Congress in Toronto. Cf. Bibliography, Nos. 5 and 56, and Selection B.

B. FEBRUARY 1955-APRIL 1959: PASTOR OF VILLA NOVA BAPTIST CHURCH (near Brantford, ON) and Missionary to Czechoslovak Immigrants in London, ON

1955   June 13: receives Canadian citizenship.

        July 12-16: Czechoslovak Baptist Convention, annual assembly in Chicago, IL.

1956-57   July 1956-August 1957: Study leave from the church for doctoral studies at the University of Zurich, Switzerland, and for research at the Baptist Theological Seminary in Ruschlikon.

1957   March 20-23: Conference of European Baptist Theological Teachers at Ruschlikon. Cf. Bibliography, No. 45, and Selection W.

1958   June 27-July 2: 5th Baptist World Youth Conference in Toronto.

1958-62   Chairperson of the Religious Liberty Committee, BFC.

III. BRANCHING OUT INTO CANADIAN BAPTIST LIFE:

DENOMINATIONAL MINISTRY, 1959-68

    May 1959-December 1963: BJA Counsellor and Assistant Superintendent, The Home Mission Board, BCOQ (with Dr. Dixon A. Burns), Toronto

    January 1964-July 1966: Assistant Secretary, Department of Canadian Missions, BCOQ, Toronto

    August 1966-June 1968: Secretary, Department of Canadian Missions, BCOQ, Toronto

1959   June: Seminar on Anabaptist Research, Elkhart and Goshen, IN.

        September: Conference on Religious Liberty, sponsored by the Baptist Joint Committee on Public Affairs, Washington, DC. Attended a series of such conferences in Washington, 1959 to 1964, 1970 and 1979.

November 2-13: Refresher Course for Ministers, sponsored by the Home Mission Board (BCOQ) and McMaster Divinity College, Hamilton, ON (lecturer).

1960 May 5-6: Conference on "Roman Catholicism: Evangelism and Religious Liberty." Sponsored by the Home Mission Board (BCOQ) and The Committee on Protestant-Roman Catholic Affairs (United Baptist Convention of the Maritime Provinces), Cambellton, NB.

July 1-4: Czechoslovak Baptist Convention, annual assembly in Campbell, OH.

November 1-17: Urban Ministers' School, Green Lake, WI (American Baptist).

1961 January to May: Associational Simultaneous Evangelism Clinics (a total of 27), BCOQ: coordinator and lecturer.

August 17-23: Home Missions Conference, Ridgecrest, NC (Southern Baptist).

November: Refresher Course for Ministers, Hamilton, ON (lecturer; cf. November 1959).

1962 March to May: Simultaneous Evangelism Crusades in various Associations, BCOQ (coordinator).

March: Ministers' Conference on Evangelism, Rochester, NY (American Baptist). Attended also in 1963 and 1964.

July 5-8: 6th Assembly of the Baptist Federation of Canada, Calgary, AB.

1963 May 2-4: City Missions Conference, Kansas City, MO (Southern Baptist).

Open Doors

July 12-26: Faith and Order Conference (World Council of Churches), Montreal (observer).

August 3-10: Atlantic Seaboard Conference on Missionary Education, Acadia University, Wolfville, NS (lecturer on urban church work).

October 28-November 8: Refresher Course for Ministers, Hamilton, ON (dean and lecturer; cf. November 1959 and 1961).

Fall: Urban Church Renewal Conferences in the ten largest cities, BCOQ (coordinator and lecturer).

1964 May 22-24: B.J.A. Jubilee Convention, Atlantic City, NJ.

July: Seminar on Anabaptist Research, Elkhart and Goshen, IN.

August 24-28: 6th Pacific Northwest International World Mission Conference, University of British Columbia, Vancouver, BC (lecturer on mission among ethnic groups) Cf. Bibliography, No. 13, and Selection D.

1965 January 1965 to January 1966: Study leave for doctoral studies at the University of Zurich, Switzerland. Final examination on January 29, 1966. Also visiting lecturer at the Baptist Theological Seminary in Ruschlikon.

April 6-9: Conference on Strategy in Evangelism, Ruschlikon, Switzerland.

1966 May 10: Baptist Ministers' Retreat (BCOQ), Hamilton, ON. Lecture: "Towards a Theology of Social Action."

June 10-13: Annual Assembly, BCOQ, Hamilton, ON: Commissioning address, "The Courage to be a Minority." Cf. Bibliography, No. 34, and Selection N.

August 6-13: National World Mission Conference, Green Lake, WI (American Baptist). Address:

Appendix II: Biographical Table

"Baptist Mission in Canada." Cf. Bibliography, No. 23.

1966-68 Member of Council, BFC; chair, Social Service Committee (1966-67).

1967 February 9-10: New Orleans Baptist Theological Seminary, New Orleans, LA: two lectures on "Baptist Work in Canada."

June 26-30: Conference on the Concept of the Believers' Church, Southern Baptist Theological Seminary, Louisville, KY. Response paper: "Who is a Believer?" Cf. Bibliography, No. 38, and Selection R.

July 6-9: 8th Assembly of the BFC, Ottawa. Address: "Pathways to Better Evangelism in the New Century." Cf. Bibliography, No. 24, and Selection F.

August 31-September 3: Annual Assembly of UBCAP, Wolfville, NS. Six addresses on the theme, "The Mission of the Church in Contemporary Society." Cf. Bibliography No. 27, and Selection I.

December 4-6: Institute on the Church in Industrial Society, Sudbury, ON.

December 27-30: Sessions of the American Historical Association and the American Society for Reformation Research, Toronto, ON (commentator).

IV. SHAPING THE DIRECTION OF CANADIAN BAPTISTS: TEACHING MINISTRY AND DENOMINATIONAL LEADERSHIP, 1968-91

1968 April 16-19: Annual Assembly of BUWC, Penticton, BC (devotional speaker).

June 14: Anabaptist Seminar in Elkhart, IN: Paper: "The Anabaptists and the Czech Brethren."

> July 1: Beginning of service as Associate Professor of Church History, Acadia Divinity College, Acadia University, Wolfville, NS.
>
> November 6: Faculty exchange lectures at Pine Hill Divinity School, Halifax, NS: "Two Chapters from the History of the Czech Reformation."

1968-91 Member of the Historical Records Committee (renamed Baptist Historical Committee) of UBCAP; chairman 1970-72 and 1977-82.

1969 May 13: *Dr. theol.* degree, University of Zurich, awarded (in absentia) after publication of the thesis. Cf. Bibliography, No. 72.

> June 13-15: Baptist Men's Conference, Braemar Lodge near Yarmouth, NS. Three addresses: "The Next Decade: Canadian Baptists at the Crossroads."

1970 June 25-28: Czechoslovak Baptist Convention, annual assembly, Toronto, ON.

> June 29-July 2: Believers' Church Conference, Chicago Theological Seminary, Chicago, IL (commentator).
>
> July 2-5: 9th Assembly of the CBF, Winnipeg, MN.
>
> August 24-28: Canadian Congress on Evangelism, Ottawa.
>
> September 11-13: Baptist Men's Retreat, Dalvay, PEI. Four addresses on the theme, "I make all things new."
>
> November 9-12: Baptist Ministers' Conference, BUWC, Sundre, AB. Four addresses on the theme, "The Ministries in the 1970's."
>
> December 27-31: Sessions of the American Historical Association and the American Society for Reformation Research, Boston, MA. Paper: "The Rise of Religious Liberty in the Czech Reformation." Cf. Bibliography, No. 78.

Appendix II: Biographical Table

1971   July 1: promoted to professor, ADC and Acadia University.

August 2-6: BWA Council meetings in Wolfville, NS. Paper: "Baptists in Canada and Cooperative Christianity." Cf. Bibliography, Nos. 58-59.

August 22-27: 4th International Congress for Luther Research, St. Louis, MO (commentator).

1971-81 and 1985-91

Director of Continuing Education, ADC.

1972-76   Dean of the Chapel, ADC.

1972   April 25-28: Lectures at Bethel Theological Seminary, St. Paul, MN. Theme: "The Religion Explosion: Patterns of Renewal in the Sixteenth Century and Today."

April 29-May 22: Research in American libraries for bibliography and inventory of sources for the Hussite movement. Sponsored by the Foundation for Reformation Research, St. Louis, MO. Phase I.

June 12-July 22: Phase II of the same research project. See Bibliography, Nos. 81-82.

1973   April 26-28: Centennial assembly of BUWC, Edmonton, AB. Theme address: "Western Baptists in Their New Century."

July 5-8: 10th assembly of the BFC, Wolfville, NS. Keynote address: "Reconciliation: A Gift and a Task."

September 21-23: Baptist Men's Conference, Wildwood Camp, near Moncton, NB. Four addresses on the theme: "Atlantic Baptists at the Crossroads."

December 27-30: Sessions of the American Society of Church History and the American Historical Association, San Francisco, CA. Paper: "The Hussite

Movement: Current Dilemmas in Interpretation and Research." Cf. Bibliography, No. 82.

1974 June 26-28: Annual meeting of the Institute of Mennonite Studies (U.S.A. and Canada), Winnipeg, MN. Paper: "The Proto-Anabaptism of the Unitas Fratrum."

December 27-30: Annual sessions of the American Society of Church History and the American Historical Association, Chicago, IL (commentator).

1975 January 21: Consortium on Reformation Studies of the Universities of Guelph and Waterloo, Waterloo, ON. Lecture: "Anabaptism in 1525: A Replay of Medieval Themes or a Prelude to the Modern Age?", and address, "Baptists and Mennonites: Alienated Cousins." Cf. Bibliography, Nos. 73 and 39.

June 5-8: Conference on Restitution, Dissent and Renewal, Pepperdine University, Malibu, CA. Paper: "Restitution and Dissent in the Late Medieval Renewal Movements." Cf. Bibliography, No. 79.

1976 January 19-23: Mennonite Brethren Bible College and Canadian Mennonite College (now Concord College), Winnipeg, MN. Lectures on "Anabaptism as a Renewal Movement."

February 16-18: Baptist Ministers' Conference (BCOQ), Cedar Glen Retreat Centre, Bolton, ON. Four addresses on the theme: "Conversations on Renewal."

May 17-20: Carey Hall (BUWC), Vancouver, BC. Lectures on the Believers' Church.

July 8-11: 11th Assembly of BFC, Hamilton, ON. Elected Vice-President, 1976-1979.

1976-77 July 1976 to June 1977: Sabbatical leave. Scholar-in-residence and adjunct professor at the Associated

Appendix II: Biographical Table

Mennonite Biblical Seminaries, Elkhart, IN. Research in the libraries of the University of Chicago and Notre Dame University for the Bibliography of the Hussite Movement, Cf. Bibliography No. 81.

1976 October 28-31: Sessions of the American Academy of Religion and the American Society for Reformation Research, St. Louis, MO. Paper: "Responses to Calvin and Calvinism among the Czech Brethren." Cf. Bibliography, No. 80.

1977 May 5-8: Conference on Medieval Studies at Western Michigan University, Kalamazoo, MI. (commentator). Attended also the same annual conferences in 1978-1980 and 1985.

1978 February 14-16: The 11th Annual Day-Higginbotham Lectures at Southwestern Baptist Theological Seminary, Ft. Worth, TX, on the theme: "Baptist Roots in the Radical Reformation." Cf. Bibliography, Nos. 74-76.

May 15-18: Study Conference on the Believers' Church in Canada, Winnipeg, MN. Chairman of the program committee, presenter of a paper, and co-editor of the conference volume. Cf. Bibliography, Nos. 40, 60 and 68, and Selection S.

July 13-16: Summer School of the Baptist Historical Society, Norwich, England. Paper: "Baptists in Canada."

July 24-29: Oxford Research Conference on Revivals (coordinator, J. Edwin Orr), Regent's Park College, Oxford, England. Paper: "The Hussite Movement as a Religious Revival."

1979 July 12-15: 12th Assembly of BFC, Regina, SK. Elected President. Address: "Believers in Expectation." Cf. Bibliography, No. 29, and Selection K.

July 23-August 10: Visiting Lecturer at Regent College, Vancouver, BC.

September 27-29: XIe Congrès des relations internationales du Québec, Québec City, on the theme: "The Church and World System: The Position of the Churches in International Affairs." Paper: "Human Rights and the Christian Peace Conference in Eastern Europe." Cf. Bibliography, No. 54.

October 15-18: International Symposium on "Baptists in Canada, 1760-1980", Acadia Divinity College, Wolfville, NS. Conference coordinator; paper, "They Speak in Other Tongues," and editor of one conference volume. Cf. Bibliography, Nos. 61 and 69.

1979-82 President of Baptist Federation of Canada.

1979-84 Member of the Advisory Committee on Religion, Canadian Broadcasting Corporation.

1979-92 Chairman, Editorial Committee for the series, "Baptist Heritage in Atlantic Canada."

1980 April 8-10: Canadian Church Leaders Conference, Pierrefonds, PQ.

June 5-8: Annual Assembly of BCOQ and BWMS, Hamilton, ON. Three addresses on the theme of growth. Cf. Bibliography, Nos. 30, 31 and 41, and Selection T.

July 8-13: 14th BWA Congress, Toronto (Words of Welcome as President of BFC).

July 17-20: Czechoslovak Baptist Convention, annual assembly in Minitonas, Manitoba. Three addresses.

October 17-20: Congress of the Czechoslovak Society of Arts and Sciences, Washington, DC (panel member).

October 21: J. R. Couillard Memorial Lectures, Moravian Theological Seminary, Bethlehem, PA. Theme: "Renewal of Church and Society in the Hussite Reformation." Cf. Bibliography, Nos. 85-86.

Appendix II: Biographical Table

October 23-25: Sixteenth Century Studies Conference, St. Louis, MO. Paper: "An Overlooked Early Plea for Believer's Baptism, 1521."

November 10-13: Baptist Ministers' Conference, BUWC, Banff, BC. Four addresses on the theme, "The Nature of the Church."

1980-82 Vice-Chairman, Commission on Human Rights, BWA.

1981 April 21-23: Canadian Church Leaders Conference, Pierrefonds, PQ. Paper: "Canadian Baptists."

November 6-7: Ecumenical Seminar on Church-State Relations in Canada, Montreal.

November 26-27: Inter-Church Committee (Canadian Church Leaders) meeting, Montreal.

December 4-5: Peace Seminar (BCOQ), Ganaraska Woods, ON (seminar leader).

1982 January 14-17: International Baptist Conference on Theological Education (sponsored by BWA), Ridgecrest, NC (panel member).

July 1-4: 13th Assembly of BFC, Moncton, NB. Presidential address: "Can God Turn the Tide?" Cf. Bibliography, No. 32, and Selection L.

July 16-August 8: Tour of historical sites related to the Reformation, in Denmark, Holland, W. Germany and Switzerland (with Dr. William H. Jones). Cf. Bibliography, No. 50.

August 17-27: Meetings of the General Council of the World Alliance of Reformed Churches, Ottawa (fraternal delegate).

1982-85 Past President of BFC, and Chairman, Inter-Church Relations Committee, BFC.

1983 May 4-25: Visiting lecturer at Gordon-Conwell Theological Seminary, South Hamilton, MA (near Boston).

June 10-12: Saskatchewan Area (BUWC), annual meetings, Prince Albert, SK. Five addresses on the theme, "Roots and Fruits."

July 24-August 10: Sixth Assembly of the World Council of Churches, Vancouver, BC (accredited visitor and reporter). Cf. Bibliography, Nos. 42-43, and Selection V.

1984 April 28-May 25: Visiting lecturer at Baptist Theological Seminary, Ruschlikon, Switzerland.

July to December: Half-sabbatical leave. Research in the Moravian Archives and Library in Bethlehem, PA.

September 25: Annual meeting of the Moravian Historical Society, Bethlehem, PA. Paper: "The Ecumenical Contacts of the Old Bohemian Brethren."

October 15-17: Baptist Heritage Conference, McMaster Divinity College, Hamilton, ON. Paper: "The Changing Baptist Identity in Canada since World War II." Cf. Bibliography, No. 63.

1985 May 14: D.D. degree from McMaster University. Convocation address, "Potential for Renewal." Cf. Bibliography, No. 33, and Selection M.

1985-90 Vice-Chairman, Commission on Baptist Heritage, BWA.

1985-91 Member of Faith and Order, Church Relations (FOCR) Committee, CBF.

1986 July and August: Research in Canadian Baptist Archives, McMaster Divinity College, Hamilton, ON and in the library of the American Baptist Historical Society in Rochester, NY, in preparation for the bibliography of Baptists in Canada. Cf. Bibliography, No. 65.

August 4-15: Visiting lecturer at the Ontario Theological Seminary, Toronto, ON.

Appendix II: Biographical Table

1987   October 19-23: Baptist Heritage Conference, Acadia Divinity College, Wolfville, NS. Conference coordinator and editor of one conference volume. Cf. Bibliography, No. 70.

1988-89 Health Problems.

1990   May 19-22: Baptist Heritage Conference, North American Baptist Seminary (now Edmonton Baptist Seminary), Edmonton, AB. Paper: "Building a Future on the Past." Cf. Bibliography, No. 67, and Selection Q.

1991   April 1: Acadia Centre for Baptist and Anabaptist Studies established by Acadia Divinity College, in cooperation with Acadia University Library; appointed honourary director of the Centre.

July 1: Retirement.

APPENDIX III
BIBLIOGRAPHY OF SELECTED POPULAR PUBLICATIONS

Note. Asterisks identify texts included in this volume.

A. Early Spiritual Pilgrimage

1.* "My Conversion and Call to Ministry." Parts 1 and 2 of "Statement before the Examining Council for Ordination", presented in Toronto, May 30, 1950. [Published in *Open Doors* (1992), Selection A.]

2. "A Canadian Czechoslovakian Pastor: The Story of the Life of Mr. J. Zeman." L & V, May 1950: 163-165. [based on an interview by the editor, Miss Alfreda Hall]

   Note. See also No. 57.

B. Canadian Baptist Heritage, Identity and Mission

Note. The categories under B. correspond to Parts Two to Seven in *Open Doors*. In each category, items are listed in chronological order.

I. Ministries Among Immigrants (New Canadians)

3. "The People Had a Mind to Work" and "A Great Day". L & V, October 1952: 309-313. [Report on the opening of Bethlehem Czechoslovak Baptist Church in Toronto, September 7, 1952; based on an interview by the editor, Miss Alfreda Hall.] Cf. also CB, October 1, 1952: 3.

4. "A Unique Gathering: New Canadian Pastors Confer." CB, December 15, 1952: 1 & 11.

5.* *Baptist Missions among Czechoslovak People in Canada.* Toronto: The Home Mission Board, BCOQ, 1954, 8 pp. [Reprinted in *Open Doors* (1992), Selection B.]

Appendix III: Popular Publications

6. "A Call to Reconsider Work Among Immigrants." L & V, May 1956: 165-167.

7. "Canadian Christian Fellowship Night, Villa Nova." L & V, January 1959: 28-29.

8. "New Canadian Pastors and Missionaries." CB, November 2, 1959: 3.

9.* Why Do Immigrants Come to Canada?" Message on CBC Radio, July 2, 1961. [Published in *Open Doors* (1992), Selection C.]

10.* "The New Approach to New Canadian Work." *Canadian Baptist Home Missions Digest* 5 (1961-1962): 196-205. Published also as a pamphlet under the same title, by The Home Mission Board, BCOQ, 1962, 12 pp. [Reprinted, in part, in *Open Doors* (1992), Selection E.] A brief summary appeared also in CB, May 1, 1962: 8.

11. "God Speaks in Many Tongues." *The Canadian Baptist Leader* (Toronto), Winter 1962: 11-14.

12. "The New Canadian Sponsorship Plan." L & V, October 1964: 272-273.

13.* *The Whole World at Our Door. The Church's Mission to Ethnic Groups in Canada: A Guide for Study and Action*. Toronto: BCOQ & BWMS, 1964, 32 pp. [Chapter II, "The Role of the Ethnic Church", reprinted in *Open Doors* (1992), Selection D.]

Note. See also No. 61.

II. Evangelism and Home Missions

14. "Norfolk Association: BJA Program Moves Ahead." CB, February 16, 1959: 1, 3 & 13.

15. "The B.J.A. Column." A monthly column in CB, from September 1, 1959 to June 1, 1960.

16. "The Mission Circle's Role in Baptist Jubilee Advance." L & V, January 1960: 4-5. [A digest of an address]

17. "Has the B.J.A. Any Meaning For Canadian Baptists?" *Canadian Baptist Home Missions Digest* 5 (1961-1962): 48-52.

18. *God's Mission and Ours: Bible Study Outlines*. Brantford: BFC, 1963, 36 pp. Reprinted in Edmonton: Strathcona Baptist Church, 1973, 36 pp. [BJA 1963 Study Book]

19. "To Conquer and to Serve: The Twofold Task of Canadian Missions." [A message delivered at Yorkminster Park Baptist Church, Toronto, November 15, 1964; mimeographed, 6 pp.]

20. "Department of Canadian Missions." A regular column in CB, 1966-1968.

21. [editor] *Church-centred Social Service*. Toronto: BCOQ, Department of Canadian Missions, 1966, 22 pp. [Transcript of a panel discussion at Yorkminster Park Baptist Church, Toronto, March 8, 1966.]

22.* "Are Canadian Baptists Interested in Social Action?" *Canadian Baptist Home Missions Digest* 7 (1966-1967): 89-91 & 97. [Reprinted in *Open Doors* (1992), Selection G.]

23. "A Canadian Baptist Viewpoint." *Impact* I/3 (March 1967): 31-35 [A publication of American Baptist Board of Education and Publications, Valley Forge, PA; abbreviated text of an address, "Baptist Mission in Canada" at Green Lake, WI, in August 1966]

24.* "Pathways to Better Evangelism in the New Country." *The Report Volume of the Eighth Assembly of the BFC, Ottawa, July 6-9, 1967*. Brantford, ON: BFC, n.d.: 53-58. [A slightly abbreviated and edited text was published also in the *Crusader* (Valley Forge, PA), January 1968: 8-9. [Reprinted in *Open Doors* (1992), Selection F.]

25.* "Dr. Jarold Zeman at Toronto B.W. Conference, March 25, 1968." L & V, May 1968: 151-152. [A summary of the address, "Two Visions", by the editor, Miss Alfreda Hall; reprinted in *Open Doors* (1992), Selection H.]

Appendix III: Popular Publications

III. Renewal and Revival in Canadian Baptist Life

26. "The Turning of the Tide." *Canadian Baptist Home Missions Digest* 4 (1959): 170-174. [the BJA program emphasis]

27.* "The Sleeping Giant." *Atlantic Baptist*, December 1, 1967: 2. [Reprinted in *Open Doors* (1992), Selection I.]

28.* "The State of the Convention (BCOQ): A Personal Submission to the Commission on the State of the Convention, March 21, 1968." (12 pp.) [Parts I, III and IV published in *Open Doors* (1992), Selection J.]

29.* "Believers in Expectation." *Expect a Difference: The Report Volume of the BFC, 1976-1979*. Brantford, ON: BFC, 1979: 50-53. [Reprinted in *Open Doors* (1992), Selection K.]

30. "Identifying Growth." CB, November 1980: 46-47.

31. "The Mystery of Growth." CB, December 1980: 4-5.

32.* "Can God Turn the Tide?" *Turning the Tide: The Report of Proceedings of the BFC, 1980-1982*. Toronto: BFC, 1982: 24-27. Published also in CB, October 1982: 52-57. [Reprinted in *Open Doors* (1992), Selection L.]

33.* "Potential for Renewal." CB, September 1985: 4-6. [Reprinted in *Open Doors* (1992), Selection M.]

IV. Canadian Baptist Heritage and Identity

34.* "The Courage to be a Minority." CB, July 1, 1966: 9, 12 & 15. [Reprinted in *Open Doors* (1992), Selection N.]

35.* "The Paradox of Baptist Origins and Destiny." Wolfville, NS, November 15, 1970 (mimeographed, 5 pp.). [Part IV reprinted in *Open Doors* (1992), Selection O.]

36.* "Authority and Freedom: A Baptist View." *Atlantic Baptist*, January 15, 1970: 1 & 13. [Reprinted in *Open Doors* (1992), Selection P.]

37. "Baptists in Canada: Basic Facts for Quick Orientation." Toronto: BFC, 1981. (mimeographed, 18 pp.)

V. Canadian Baptists in the Wider Ecumenical Context

38.* "The Believers' Church: Who is a Believer?" (Response at the Believers' Church Conference in Louisville, KY, 1957; mimeographed, 5 pp.) [Reprinted in *Open Doors* (1992), Selection R.]

39. "Baptists and Mennonites: Alienated Cousins." *Mennonite Reporter* (Waterloo, ON), August 15, 1975: 5.

40.* "The Significance of the Concept of the Believers' Church." (Statement in preparation for the Believers' Church Conference in Winnipeg, May 1978; mimeographed, 1977, 2 pp.) [Reprinted in *Open Doors* (1992), Selection S.]

41.* "Growing Together." CB, October 1980: 4-6. [Reprinted, in part, in *Open Doors* (1992), Selection T.]

42.* "Report and Reflections on the Sixth Assembly of the World Council of Churches in Vancouver, BC, July 24-August 10, 1983." (mimeographed, 1983, 15 pp.) [Sections 2 and 6 reprinted in *Open Doors* (1992), Selection V.]

43. "Which Road After Vancouver?" *Bulletin of the Atlantic Baptist Fellowship*, February-March 1984: 9-12.

44.* "Interfaith Interface." CB, October 1984: 14-15 & 31. [Reprinted in *Open Doors* (1992), Selection U.]

Note. See also No. 24 ("Pathways to Better Evangelism"), Part I. 5 (Social and Theological Ecumenicity).

VI. Ministry and Ministerial Training

45.* "How to Train Good Ministers." CB, May 15, 1957: 7 & 11. [Reprinted in *Open Doors* (1992), Selection W.]

46.* "Partnership in Ministries." CB, September 1987: 4-6. [Reprinted in *Open Doors* (1992), Selection X.]

47.* "A Plea for Wholeness in Theological Education." (1990). [Published in *Open Doors* (1992), Selection Y.]

Appendix III: Popular Publications

C. Reformation History and Heritage

48. "Which Reformation? A Question for Reformation Sunday." CB, October 15, 1959: 8 & 13.
49. "Reformation: Relevant?" *Atlantic Baptist*, October 15, 1969: 1, 4 & 10.
50. "Questions That Remain: Perspectives on the Reformation." CB, November 1982: 4-8.

D. Miscellaneous

51. "European Leaders Oppose Rearmament." *United Church Observer*, May 15, 1951. [Karl Barth, Joseph L. Hromadka and Martin Niemoeller]
52. "Haiti—The Country of God", and other sections, in *"Go Ye ...": Mission Fields of The Czechoslovak Baptist Convention of the U.S.A. and Canada*. Compiled by V. P. Stupka. (Chicago: The Czechoslovak Baptist Convention, n.d. [1952]), 63 pp. [impressions from a visit to Haiti in July 1951]
53. "Abiding in Christian Hope." Ch. 7 in *Journey in Life: Seven Studies in Christian Experience*. Edited by Theo T. Gibson. (Saint John, NB: UBCAP, 1969), pp. 50-56.
54. "Human Rights and the Christian Peace Conference in Eastern Europe." *Eglise et système mondial—The Church and World System*. Edited by A. Jacomy-Millette et al. (Québec: Université Laval, 1980), pp. 165-171.

E. Popular Publications in the Czech Language

55. [Editor and contributor] *Betlemsky kostel, Toronto, Canada: Pametni spis ... u prilezitosti otevreni, 7 September 1952*. (Toronto: Czechoslovak Baptist Church, 1952), 32 pp. [A Program Book, with historical articles, for the dedication of Bethlehem Baptist Church, 17 Rhodes Ave., Toronto]
56. [Editor and contributor] *Narode muj, ziv bud' v Bohu! Program of the Czechoslovak Baptist Congress, Toronto, July 2-*

8, 1954. (Toronto: Czechoslovak Baptist Church, 1954), 48 pp. [articles in Czech and English]

57. *Krest a cirkev: Proc jsem se stal baptistou?* (Chicago—Toronto: Edice Pravdy, 1956), 32 pp. [Baptism and Church: Why I Became a Baptist] [incl. a brief review of the ecumenical discussions of baptism in the 1940s and early 1950s]

Note. Several articles were published, during the student days in Prague, in the Protestant periodicals *Bratrstvo* and *Kostnicke jiskry* (1946-1947). During the years 1949-1968, many articles appeared in the Czech secular papers *Novy domov* (Toronto) and *Nase hlasy* (Toronto), and in the religious periodicals, *Husuv lid*, *Krest'anske listy* and *Pravda a Slavna Nadeje*, all published by Czechoslovak Protestant organizations in the U.S.A.

From 1949 to 1954, additional popular articles appeared in two Czech papers, started and edited by J.K.Z., in Toronto: *Cesta zivota* [The Way of Life] and *Bozi zitrek* [God's Tomorrow].

F. A Note re the Original Text of Selections Published in this Volume

In several selections which are reprinted in this volume, or published here for the first time, some sections of the text were deleted. Such deletions are indicated by editorial notes in the text. The complete original text of such selections has been deposited in the Atlantic Baptist Collection, Acadia University Archives/Library, under the label: "Zeman—Open Doors."

APPENDIX IV

BIBLIOGRAPHY OF SELECTED SCHOLARLY PUBLICATIONS

A. Canadian Baptist History and Identity

58. "Baptists in Canada and Cooperative Christianity." *Foundations* 15 (1972): 211-240. Also a separate edition, published by BFC, 1972, 30 pp.

59. "Canada." Chapter 10 in *Baptist Relations with Other Christians*. Ed. James Leo Garrett. (Valley Forge: Judson Press, 1974), pp. 105-119. [an abbreviated text of No. 58]

60. "The Believers' Church: Canadian Focus." Chapter 2 in *The Believers' Church in Canada* (1979), pp. 17-24. See No. 68.

61. "They Speak in Other Tongues: Witness Among Immigrants." Chapter 4 in *Baptists in Canada* (1980), pp. 67-86. See No. 69.

62. "Canadian Baptists." *Encyclopedia of Southern Baptists*, vol. 4 (Nashville: Broadman Press, 1982).

63. "The Changing Baptist Identity in Canada since World War II." *Celebrating the Canadian Baptist Heritage*. Ed. Paul R. Dekar and M. J. S. Ford. (Hamilton, ON: McMaster Divinity College, n.d. [1984], pp. 1-26.

64. "Baptists." *The Canadian Encyclopedia*, vol. 1 (Edmonton: Hurtig Publishers, 1985; 2nd rev. ed., 1989).

65. *Baptists in Canada 1760-1990: A Bibliography of Selected Printed Resources in English*. Prepared by Philip G. A. Griffin-Allwood, George A. Rawlyk and Jarold K. Zeman. (Hantsport, NS: Lancelot Press, 1989), xx & 266 pp.

66. "Baptists in Canada." *Dictionary of Christianity in America*. Ed. Daniel G. Reid and others. (Downers Grove, IL: InterVarsity Press, 1990).

Open Doors

67.* "Building a Future on the Past." *McMaster Journal of Theology*, vol. 1, No. 2 (Fall 1990): 56-67. Reprinted in *Memory and Hope*. Ed. David B. Priestley (Burlington, ON: Welch Publishing Co., 1991). [The last section is reprinted in *Open Doors* (1992), Selection Q.]

Note. See also No. 75, *Baptist Roots and Identity*, Chapter 6.

Editorial Work

68. *The Believers' Church in Canada.* Ed. J. K. Zeman and W. Klaassen. (N. p.: Baptist Federation of Canada and Mennonite Central Committee, 1979), xv & 410 pp.
69. *Baptists in Canada: Search for Identity Amidst Diversity.* Ed. J. K. Zeman. (Burlington, ON: G. R. Welch, 1980), x & 282 pp.
70. *Costly Vision: The Baptist Pilgrimage in Canada.* Ed. J. K. Zeman. (Burlington, ON: Welch Publishing Co., 1988), xiv & 282 pp.

Note. Chairperson of the Editorial Committee for the series, "Baptist Heritage in Atlantic Canada (Documents and Studies)." (Hantsport, NS: Lancelot Press). Eleven volumes published, 1979-1989.

B. Reformation History and Theology: Anabaptism

71. "Historical Topography of Moravian Anabaptism." *The Mennonite Quarterly Review* 40 (1966): 266-278, and 41 (1967): 40-78 and 116-160. Also a separate edition, published by the Mennonite Historical Society for Goshen College, Goshen, IN, 1967, 99 pp.
72. *The Anabaptists and the Czech Brethren in Moravia, 1526-1628.* (The Hague-Paris: Mouton , 1969), 407 pp. [revised text of the doctoral dissertation, University of Zurich, 1966]
73. "Anabaptism: A Replay of Medieval Themes or a Prelude to the Modern Age?" *The Mennonite Quarterly Review* 50 (1976): 259-271.

Appendix IV: Scholarly Publications

74. "Baptist Roots in the Radical Reformation." Mimeographed text of The Day - Higginbotham Lectures at the Southwestern Baptist Theological Seminary, Fort Worth, TX, February 14-16, 1978. [the text as delivered; circulated by the Seminary]

75. *Baptist Roots and Identity*. Toronto: BCOQ, 1978, 43 pp. [Chapters I - III are the revised text of No. 74]

76. "Obedience to Christ: The Heart of Evangelical Anabaptism." *Southwestern Journal of Theology*, vol. 21, no. 2 (Spring 1979): 41-53. [revised text of the third lecture in Fort Worth, TX; see No. 74 above]

C. The Czech Reformation (The Hussite Movement)

77. *Kolebka nabozenske svobody na Morave*. (Chicago-Toronto: Edice Pravdy, 1962), 16 pp. [The Cradle of Religious Liberty in Moravia]

78. "The Rise of Religious Liberty in the Czech Reformation." *Central European History* (Atlanta, GA: Emory University) 6 (1973): 128-147.

79. "Restitution and Dissent in the Late Medieval Renewal Movements." *Journal of the American Academy of Religion* 44 (1976): 7-27.

80. "Responses to Calvin and Calvinism among the Czech Brethren." *Occasional Papers of the American Society for Reformation Research*, vol. 1 (1977): 41-52.

81. *The Hussite Movement and the Reformation in Bohemia, Moravia and Slovakia, 1350-1650: A Bibliographical Study Guide*. (Ann Arbor, MI: The University of Michigan, 1977), xxxv & 390 pp.

82. "The Hussite Movement: Trends in Interpretation and Resources for Research (particularly in North America)." The text of Introduction in *The Hussite Movement...* (No. 81), pp. xiii-xxiii.

83. "Bohemian Brethren." *Dictionary of the Middle Ages*, vol. 2. (New York: Charles Scribner's Sons, 1982).

84. Ten biographical articles in *Contemporaries of Erasmus: A Biographical Register*. Ed. P. G. Bietenholz. (Toronto: University of Toronto Press, vols. 1 (1985) and 2 (1986)). [biographies of persons in Bohemia and Moravia]
85. *Renewal of Church and Society in the Hussite Reformation. (The Couillard Memorial Lectures 1980)*. (Bethlehem, PA: Moravian Theological Seminary, 1984), 30 pp.
86. "Renewal of the Church in the Hussite Reformation" and "The Role of the Church in the Renewal of Society". *The Bulletin of the Moravian Theological Seminary, Academic Years 1977-1985*: 7-30. [the same text as No. 85]

D. Book Reviews

Reviews of scholarly books in the fields of Baptist and Anabaptist studies, as well as of the Czech Reformation, and Modern history, were published, among others, in the following journals: *Canadian Journal of Theology*; *East Central Europe*; *Fides et Historia*; *Journal of Church and State*; *Mennonite Quarterly Review*; *Sixteenth Century Journal*; *Slavic Review*; *Southwestern Journal of Theology*; and *University of Toronto Quarterly*.

PICTORIAL APPENDIX

Childhood and Youth in Czechoslovakia (1926-1948)

Top: The Reformed (Presbyterian) Church, manse (left) and school (right) buildings in Semonice (home, 1926-45).
Bottom: with younger brother John, in June 1938.

A Growing Family in Ontario
(1953-1968)

Top: with Lillian and first daughter, Miriam, in Toronto, March 1953.
Bottom: the whole family in 1968.

Professor at Acadia Divinity College (1968-1991)

Top: a newcomer at ADC (1968).
Bottom: after ten years at ADC (1978; photo: Jeff Wilson).

Preacher and Lecturer Across Canada, and Beyond

Top: at the BFC Assembly in 1973 (photo: William H. Jones).
Bottom: in the pulpit (1987).

Lillian, a Loving Companion and a Wise Counsellor

Top: early years in Wolfville (photo: Jeff Wilson).
Bottom: at the ADC Retirement Banquet (April 1991) with Dr. Robert Wilson.

The Last Evening Class at ADC: cross-cultural, cross-denominational and cross-generational (March 1991)